ISBN 978-1-330-33087-6
PIBN 10029805

This book is a reproduction of an important historical work. Forgotten Books uses state-of-the-art technology to digitally reconstruct the work, preserving the original format whilst repairing imperfections present in the aged copy. In rare cases, an imperfection in the original, such as a blemish or missing page, may be replicated in our edition. We do, however, repair the vast majority of imperfections successfully; any imperfections that remain are intentionally left to preserve the state of such historical works.

1 MONTH OF
FREE
READING

at
www.ForgottenBooks.com

By purchasing this book you are eligible for one month membership to ForgottenBooks.com, giving you unlimited access to our entire collection of over 700,000 titles via our web site and mobile apps.

To claim your free month visit: www.forgottenbooks.com/free29805

English
Français
Deutsche
Italiano
Español
Português

www.forgottenbooks.com

Mythology Photography **Fiction**
Fishing Christianity **Art** Cooking
Essays Buddhism Freemasonry
Medicine **Biology** Music **Ancient
Egypt** Evolution Carpentry Physics
Dance Geology **Mathematics** Fitness
Shakespeare **Folklore** Yoga Marketing
Confidence Immortality Biographies
Poetry **Psychology** Witchcraft
Electronics Chemistry History **Law**
Accounting **Philosophy** Anthropology
Alchemy Drama Quantum Mechanics
Atheism Sexual Health **Ancient History**
Entrepreneurship Languages Sport
Paleontology Needlework Islam
Metaphysics Investment Archaeology
Parenting Statistics Criminology
Motivational

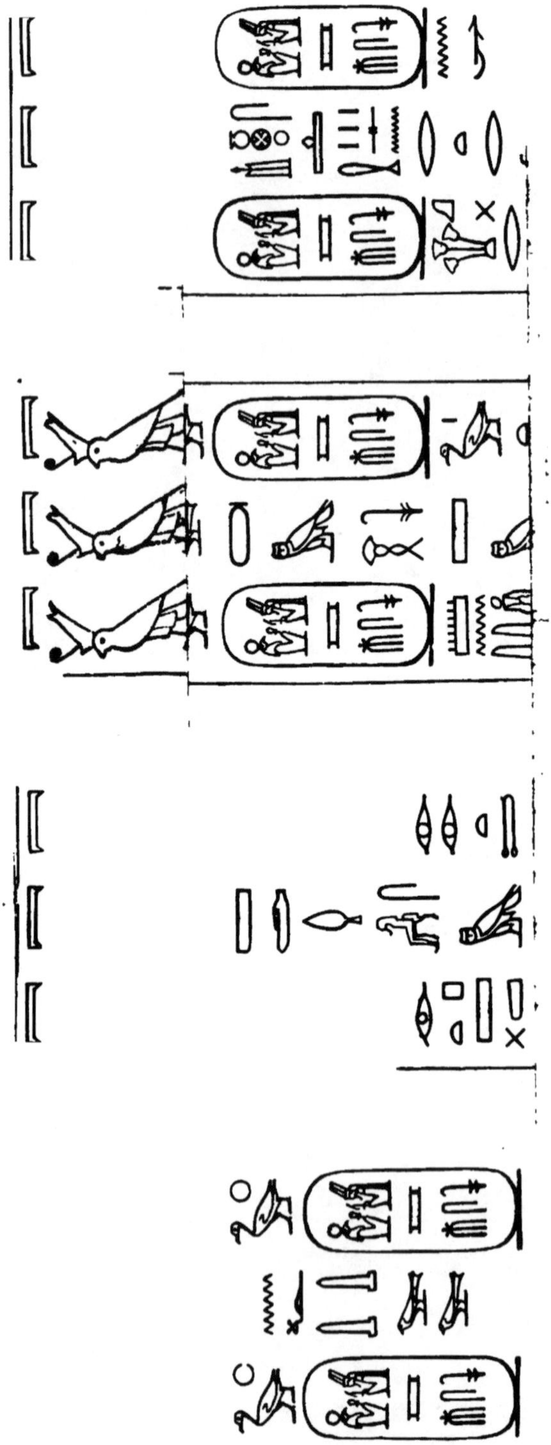

By-Paths of Bible Knowledge

I

CLEOPATRA'S NEEDLE

A HISTORY OF THE LONDON OBELISK

WITH AN

EXPOSITION OF THE HIEROGLYPHICS

BY THE

REV. JAMES KING, M.A.

AUTHORIZED LECTURER TO THE PALESTINE EXPLORATION FUND.

"The Land of Egypt is before thee."—*Gen.* xlvii. 6.

THIRD EDITION.

THE RELIGIOUS TRACT SOCIETY,

56, PATERNOSTER ROW, AND 65, ST. PAUL'S CHURCHYARD.

1886.

CONTENTS.

———o———

A 2

LIST OF ILLUSTRATIONS.

[The illustrations of the obelisk at Constantinople, and of Cleopatra's Needle on the Embankment, are taken, by the kind permission of Sir Erasmus Wilson, from his work, " The Egypt of the Past."]

INTRODUCTION.

THE London Obelisk, as the monument standing on the Thames Embankment is now called, is by far the largest quarried stone in England; and the mysterious-looking characters covering its four faces were carved by workmen who were contemporaries of Moses and the Israelites during the time of the Egyptian Bondage. It was set up before the great temple of the sun at Heliopolis about 1450 B.C., by Thothmes III., who also caused to be carved the central columns of hieroglyphs on its four sides. The eight lateral columns were carved by Rameses II. two centuries afterwards. These two monarchs were the two mightiest of the kings of ancient Egypt.

In 1877 the author passed through the land of Egypt, and became much interested during the progress of the journey in the study of the hieroglyphs covering tombs, temples, and obelisks. He was assisted in the pursuit of Egyptology by examining the excellent collections of Egyptian antiquities in the Boolak Museum at Cairo, the Louvre at Paris, and the British Museum. He feels much indebted to Dr. Samuel Birch, the leading English Egyptologist, for his kind assistance in rendering some obscure passages on the Obelisk.

This little volume contains a *verbatim* translation into English, and an exposition, of the hieroglyphic inscriptions cut by Thothmes III. on the Obelisk, and an exposition of those inscribed by Rameses II. Dr. Samuel Birch, the late W. R. Cooper, and other Egyptologists, have translated the inscription in general terms, but no attempt was made by these learned men to show the value of each hieroglyph ; ·so that the student could no more hope to gain from these general translations a knowledge of Egyptology, than he could hope to gain a knowledge of the Greek language by reading the English New Testament.

In the march of civilisation, Egypt took the lead of all the nations of the earth. The Nile Valley is a vast museum of Egyptian antiquities, and in this sunny vale search must be made for the germs of classical art.

The London Obelisk is interesting to the architect as a specimen of the masonry of a people accounted as the great builders of the Ancient World. It is interesting to the antiquary as setting forth the workmanship of artists who lived in the dim twilight of antiquity. It is interesting to the Christian because this same venerable monument was known to Moses and the Children of Israel during their sojourn in the land of Goshen.

The inscription is not of great h'storical value, but the hieroglyphs are valuable in setting forth the earliest stages of written language, while their expressive symbolism enables us to interpret the moral and religious thoughts of men who lived in the infancy of the world.

Egypt is a country of surpassing interest to the Biblical student. From the early days of patriarchal history down to the discovery in 1883 of the site of Pithom, a city founded by Rameses II., Egyptian and Israelitish and Christian history have touched at many points. Abraham visited the Nile Valley; Joseph, the slave, became lord of the whole country; God's people suffered there from cruel bondage, but the Lord so delivered them that "Egypt was glad at their departing;" the rulers of Egypt once and again ravaged Palestine, and laid Jerusalem under tribute. When, in the fulness of time, our Saviour appeared to redeem the world by the sacrifice of Himself, He was carried as a little child into Egypt, and there many of His earliest and most vivid impressions were received. Thus, from the time of Abraham, the father of the faithful, to the advent of Jesus, the Lord and Saviour of all, Egypt is associated with the history of human redemption.

And although the Obelisk which forms the subject of this volume tells us in its inscriptions nothing about Abraham, Joseph, or Moses, yet it serves among other important ends one of great interest. It seems to bring us into very direct relationship with these men who lived so many generations ago. The eyes of Moses must have rested many times upon this ancient monument, old even when first he looked upon it, and read its story of past greatness; the toiling, suffering Israelites looked upon it, and we seem to come into a closer fellowship with them as we realize this fact.

The recent wonderful discovery of mummies and Egyptian antiquities, of which an account is given in this volume, and the excavations now being carried on at Pithom and Zoan, are exciting much fresh interest in Egyptian research.

This little volume will have served its end if it interests the reader in the historical associations of the monument, which he can visit, if he cares to do so, and by its aid read for himself what it has to tell us of the men and deeds of a long-distant past.

It also seeks to stimulate wider interest and research into all that the monuments of Egypt can tell us in confirmation of the historical parts of the Bible, and of the history of that wondrous country which is prominent in the forefront of both Old and New Testaments, from the day when "Abram went down into Egypt to sojourn there," until the day when Joseph "arose and took the young Child and His mother by night, and departed into Egypt: and was there until the death of Herod: that it might be fulfilled which was spoken of the Lord by the prophet, saying, Out of Egypt have I called My Son."

CLEOPATRA'S NEEDLE.

———o———

CHAPTER I.

THE RELIGIOUS CHARACTER OF THE ANCIENT' EGYPTIANS.

STANDING some time ago on the top of the great pyramid, the present writer gazed with wonder at the wide prospect around. Above Cairo the Nile Valley is hemmed in on both sides by limestone ridges, which form barriers between the fertile fields and the barren wastes on either side ; and on the limestone ridge by the edge of the great western desert stand the pyramids of Egypt. Looking forth from the summit of the pyramid of Cheops eastwards, the Nile Valley was spread out like a panorama. The distant horizon was bounded by the Mokattam hills, and near to them rose the lofty minarets and mosques of Grand Cairo.

The green valley presented a pleasing picture of richness and industry. Palms, vines, and sycamores beautified the fertile fields; sowers, reapers, builders, hewers of wood and drawers of water plied their busy labours, while long lines of camels, donkeys, and oxen moved to and fro, laden with the rich products of the country. The hum of labour, the lowing of cattle, the bleating of sheep, the song of women, and the merry laughter of children, spoke of peace and plenty.

Looking towards the west how changed was the scene! The eye rested only on the barren sands of the vast desert, the great land of a silence unbroken by the sound of man or beast. Neither animal nor vegetable life exists there, and the solitude of desolation reigns for ever supreme; so that while the bountiful fields speak of activity and life, the boundless waste is a fitting emblem of rest and death.

It is manifest that this striking contrast exercised a strong influence upon the minds of the ancient Egyptians. To the edge of the silent desert they carried their dead for burial, and on the rocky platform that forms the margin of the sandy waste they reared those vast tombs known as the pyramids. The very configuration of Egypt preached a never-ending sermon, which intensified the moral feelings of the people, and tended to make the ancient Egyptians a religious nation.

The ancient Egyptians were a very religious people. The fundamental doctrine of their religion was the unity of deity, but this unity was never represented by any outward figure. The attributes of this being were personified and represented under positive forms. To all those not initiated into the mysteries of religion, the outward figures came to be regarded as distinct gods; and thus, in process of time, the doctrine of divine unity developed into a system of idolatry. Each spiritual attribute in course of time was represented by some natural object, and in this way nature worship became a marked characteristic of their mythology.

The sun, the most glorious object of the universe, became the central object of worship, and occupies a conspicuous position in their religious system. The various aspects of the sun as it pursued its course across the sky became so many solar deities. Horus was the youthful sun seen in the eastern horizon. He is usually represented as holding in one hand the stylus or iron pen, and in the other, either a notched stick or a tablet. In the hall of judgment, Thoth was said to stand by the dreadful balance where souls were weighed against truth. Thoth, with his iron pen, records on his tablet the result of the weighing in the case of each soul, and whether or not, when weighed in the balance, it is found wanting. According to mythology, Thoth was the child of Kneph, the ram-headed god of Thebes.

Ra or Phra was the mid-day sun ; Osiris the declining sun ; Tum or Atum the setting sun ; and Amun the sun after it had sunk below the horizon. Ptah, a god of the first order, worshipped with great magnificence at Memphis, represented the vivifying power of the sun's rays : hence Ptah is spoken of as the creative principle, and creator of all living things. Gom, Moui, and Khons, were the sons of the sun-god, and carried messages to mankind. In these we notice the rays personified. Pasht, literally a lioness, the goddess with the lioness head, was the female personification of the sun's rays.

The moon also as well as the sun was worshipped, and lunar deities received divine adoration as well as solar deities.

Thoth, the reputed inventor of hieroglyphs and the recorder of human actions, was a human deity, and represented both the light moon and the dark moon. He is also called Har and Haremakhu—the Harmachis of Greek writers—and is the personification of the vigorous young sun, the conqueror of night, who each

THOTH.

morning rose triumphant from the realms of darkness. He was the son of Isis and Osiris, and is the avenger of his father. Horus appears piercing with his spear the monster Seth or Typho, the malignant principle of darkness who had swallowed up the setting sun. The parable of the sun rising was designed to teach the great religious

lesson of the final triumph of spiritual light over darkness, and the ultimate victory of life over death.   Horus
is represented at the coronation of kings, and, together
with Seth, places the double crown upon the royal head,
saying: "Put this cap upon your head, like your father
Amen-Ra."   Princes are distinguished by a lock of hair
hanging from the side of the head, which lock is em-
blematic of a son.   This lock was worn in imitation of
Horus, who, from his strong filial affection, was a model
son for princes, and a pattern of royal virtue.   The
sphinx is thought to be a type of Horus, and the obelisks
also seem to have been dedicated, for the most part, to
the rising sun.

  There were also sky divinities, and these were all
feminine.   Nu was the blue mid-day sky, while Neit was
the dark sky of night.   Hathor or Athor, the "Queen
of Love," the Egyptian Venus, represented the evening
sky.

  There were other deities and objects of worship not so
easily classified.   Hapi was the personification of the
river Nile.   Anubis, the jackal-headed deity, was the
friend and guardian of the souls of good men.   Thmei
or Ma, the goddess of truth, introduced departed souls
into the hall of judgment.

  Amenti, the great western desert, in course of time
was applied to the unknown world beyond the desert.
Through the wilderness of Amenti departed spirits
had to pass on their way to the judgment hall.   In this
desert were four evil spirits, enemies of the human soul,

who endeavoured to delude the journeying spirits by drawing them aside from the way that led to the abode of the gods. On many papyri, and on the walls of tombs, scenes of the final judgment are frequently depicted. Horus is seen conducting the departed spirits to the regions of Amenti ; a monstrous dog, resembling Cerberus of classic fable, is guardian of the judgment hall. Near to the gates stand the dreadful scales of justice. On one side of the scales stands Thoth, the recorder of human actions, with a tablet in his hand, ready to make a record of the sentence passed on each soul. Anubis is the director of the weights ; in one scale he places the heart of the deceased, and in the other a figure of the goddess of truth. If on being weighed the heart is found wanting, then Osiris, the judge of the dead, lowers his sceptre in token of condemnation, and pronounces judgment against the soul, condemned to return to earth under the form of a pig. Whereupon the soul is placed in a boat and conveyed through Amenti under charge of two monkeys. If the deeds done in the flesh entitle the soul to enter the mansions of the blest, then Horus, taking the tablet from Thoth, introduces the good spirit into the presence of Osiris, who, with crook and flagellum in his hands, and attended by his sister Isis, with overspreading wings, sits on a throne rising from the midst of the waters. The approved soul is then admitted to the mansions of the blest.

To this belief in a future life, the custom among the

Egyptians of embalming the dead was due. Each man as he died hoped to be among those who, after living for three thousand years with Osiris, would return to earth and re-enter their old bodies. So they took steps to ensure the preservation of the body against the ravages of time, and entombed them in massive sarcophagi and in splendid sepulchres. So well did they ensure this end that when, a few months ago, human eyes looked upon the face of Thothmes III., more than three thousand years after his body had been embalmed, it was only the sudden crumbling away of the form on exposure to the air, that recalled to the remembrance of the onlookers the many ages that had passed since men last saw that face.

It is with the worship of the sun that the obelisk now on the Embankment is associated, as it stood for many ages before one of the great temples at Heliopolis, the Biblical On.

Impressive as this ancient Egyptian religious life was, it cannot be compared for a moment, judged even on the earthly standard of its moral power, to the monotheism and the religious life afterwards revealed to the Hebrews, when emancipated from Egyptian bondage. The religion first made known through God's intercourse with the Patriarchs, continued by Moses and the Prophets, and culminating in the incarnation and death of Christ the Lord, lacks much of the outward splendour and magnificence of the Egyptian religion, but satisfies infinitely better the hearts of weary sinful men.

The Egyptian worship and religious life testify to a constant degradation in the popular idea of the gods and in the moral life of their worshippers. The worship and religious life of which the God of the Hebrews is the centre, tends ever more and more to lead men in that "path of the just, which is as the shining light, that shineth more and more unto the perfect day."* Now in Christ Jesus those that once "were far off are made nigh by the blood of Christ."† "The times of ignorance" are now past, and God "commandeth men that they should all everywhere repent: inasmuch as He hath appointed a day in the which He will judge the world in righteousness by that Man whom He hath ordained." ‡

* Prov. iv. 18.   † Eph. ii. 13.   ‡ Acts xvii. 30, 31.

♪

CHAPTER II.

OBELISKS, AND THE OBELISK FAMILY

AN obelisk is a single upright stone with four sides slightly inclined towards each other. It generally stands upon a square base or pedestal, also a single stone. The pedestal itself is often supported upon two broad, deep steps. The top of the obelisk resembles a small pyramid, called a pyramidion, the sides of which are generally inclined at an angle of sixty degrees. The obelisks of the Pharaohs are made of red granite called Syenite.

In the quarries at Syene may yet be seen an unfinished obelisk, still adhering to the native rock, with traces of the workmen's tools so clearly seen on its surface, that one might suppose they had been suddenly called away, and intended soon to return to finish their work. This unfinished obelisk shows the mode in which the ancients separated these immense monoliths from the native rock. In a sharply cut groove marking the boundary of the stone are holes, evidently designed for wooden wedges. After these had been firmly driven into the holes, the groove was filled with water. The wedges gradually absorbing the water, swelled, and cracked the granite throughout the length of the groove.

The block once detached from the rock, was pushed

B

forwards upon rollers made of the stems of palm-trees, from the quarries to the edge of the Nile, where it was surrounded by a large timber raft. It lay by the river-side until the next inundation of the Nile, when the rising waters floated the raft and conveyed the obelisk down the stream to the city where it was to be set up. Thousands of willing hands pushed it on rollers up an inclined plane to the front of the temple where it was designed to stand. The pedestal had previously been placed in position, and a firm causeway of sand covered with planks led to the top of it. Then, by means of rollers, levers, and ropes made of the date-palm, the obelisk was gradually hoisted into an upright position. It speaks much for the mechanical accuracy of the Egyptian masons, that so true was the level of the top of the base and the bottom of the long shaft, that in no single instance has the obelisk been found to be out of the true perpendicular.

There has not yet been found on the bas-reliefs or paintings any representation of the transport of an obelisk, although there is sufficient external evidence to prove that the foregoing mode was the usual one. In a grotto at El Bersheh, however, is a well-known representation of the transportation of a colossal figure from the quarries. The colossus is mounted on a huge sledge, and as a man is represented pouring oil in front of the sledge, it would appear that on the road prepared for its transport there was a sliding groove along which the colossus was propelled. Four long rows of men, urged

OBELISK OF USERTESEN I., STILL STANDING AT HELIOPOLIS.

on in their work by taskmasters, are dragging the figure by means of ropes.

The Syenite granite was very hard, and capable of taking a high polish. The carving is very beautifully executed, and the hieroglyphs rise from a sunken surface, in a style known as "incavo relievo." In this mode of carving the figures never project beyond the surface of the stone, and consequently are not so liable to be chipped off as they would have been had they projected in "high relief." The hieroglyphs are always arranged on the obelisks with great taste, in long vertical columns, and these were always carved after the obelisk was placed in its permanent position.

The hewing, transport, hoisting, and carving of such a monolith was a gigantic undertaking, and we are not therefore surprised to learn that "the giant of the obelisk race," now in front of St. John Lateran, Rome, occupied the workmen thirty-six years in its elaboration.

The chief obelisks known, taking them in chronological order, are as follows:—Three were erected by Usertesen I., a monarch of the XIIth dynasty, who lived about 1750 B.C. He is thought by some to be the Pharaoh that promoted Joseph. Of these three obelisks one still stands at Heliopolis in its original position, and from its great age it has been called "the father of obelisks." It is sixty-seven and a-half feet high, and is therefore about a foot shorter than the London obelisk. Its companion is missing, and probably lies buried amid the ruins of the sacred city. The third is at Biggig, in the Fyoom, and, unfortunately, is broken into two parts. Its shape is peculiar, and on that account Bonomi and others say that it cannot with propriety be classed among the obelisks.

After the XIIth dynasty Egypt was ruled for many centuries by monarchs of Asiatic origin, called the Hykshos or "Shepherd Kings." During the rule of those foreigners it does not appear that any obelisks were erected.

Thothmes I., of the XVIIIth dynasty, erected two in front of the Osiris temple at Karnak. One of these is still standing, the other lies buried by its side. Hatasu, daughter of Thothmes I, and queen of Egypt, erected two obelisks inside the Osiris temple of Karnak, in honour of her father. One, still standing, is about one hundred feet high, and is the second highest obelisk in the world. Its companion has fallen to the ground. According to Mariette Bey, Hatasu erected two other obelisks in front of her own temple on the western bank of the Nile. These, however, have been destroyed, although the pedestals still remain.

Thothmes III., the greatest of Egyptian monarchs, and brother of Hatasu, erected four obelisks at Heliopolis, and probably others in different parts of Egypt. These four have been named "The Needles"—two of them "Pharaoh's Needles," and two "Cleopatra's Needles." The former pair were removed from Heliopolis to Alexandria by Constantine the Great. Thence one was taken, according to some Egyptologists, to Constantinople, where it now stands at the Atmeidan. It is only fifty feet high, but it is thought that the lower part has been broken off, and that the part remaining is only the upper half of the original obelisk.

THE OBELISK OF THOTHMES III., AT CONSTANTINOPLE.

The other was conveyed to Rome, and now stands in front of the church of St. John Lateran, and from its great magnitude it is regarded as "the giant of the obelisk family."

Amenophis II., of the XVIIIth dynasty, set up a small obelisk, of Syenite granite, about nine feet high. It was found amid the ruins of a village of the Thebaid, and presented to the late Duke of Northumberland, then Lord Prudhoe.

Amenophis III., of the XVIIIth dynasty, erected two obelisks in front of his temple at Karnak; but the temple is in ruins, and the obelisks have entirely disappeared.

Seti I. set up two; one, known as the Flaminian obelisk, now stands at the Porta del Popolo, Rome, and the other at Trinita de Monti, in the same city.

Rameses II. was, next to Thothmes III., the mightiest king of Egypt; and in the erection of obelisks he surpassed all other monarchs. He set up two obelisks before the temple of Luxor; one is still standing, but the other was transported to Paris about forty years ago. The latter is seventy-six feet high, and seven and a-half feet higher than the London one. Two obelisks, bearing the name of Rameses II., are at Rome, one in front of the Pantheon, the other on the Cœlian Hill.

Ten obelisks, the work of the same monarch, lie buried at Tanis, the ancient Zoan.

Menephtah, son and successor of Rameses, set up the obelisk which now stands in front of St. Peter's, Rome. It is about ninety feet high, and as regards magnitude is the third obelisk in the world.

Psammeticus I., of the XXVIth dynasty, set up an obelisk at Heliopolis in the year 665 B.C. It now stands at Rome on the Monte Citorio. Psammeticus II., about the same time that Solomon's temple was destroyed, erected an obelisk which now stands at Rome, on the back of an elephant. Nectanebo I. made two small obelisks of black basalt. They are now in the British Museum, and, according to Dr. Birch, were dedicated to Thoth, the Egyptian god of letters. They were found at Cairo, built into the walls of some houses. One was used as a door-sill, the other as a window-sill. They came into possession of the English when the French in Egypt capitulated to the British, and were presented to the British Museum by King George III. in 1801. They are only eight feet high.

Nectanebo II., of the XXXth dynasty, who lived about four centuries before the Christian era, set up two obelisks. One hundred years afterwards they were placed by Ptolemy Philadelphus in front of the tomb of his wife Arsinoë. They were taken to Rome, and set up before the mausoleum of Augustus, where they stood till the destruction of the city in 450 A.D. They lay buried amid the *débris* of Rome for many hundreds of years, but about a century ago they were dug out. One now stands behind the Church of St. Maria Maggiore, the other in the Piazza Quirinale. Each is about fifty feet high.

Two large obelisks were transported from Egypt to Nineveh in 664 B.C. by Assurbanipal. These two mono-liths probably lie buried amid the ruins of that ancient city. The above include the chief obelisks erected by the Pharaohs; but several others were erected by the Roman Emperors. Domitian set up one thirty-four feet high, which now stands in the Piazza Navona, in front of

the Church of St. Agnes.   Domitian and Titus erected
a small obelisk of red granite nine feet high, which
now stands in the cathedral square of Benevento.
Hadrian and Sabina set up two obelisks, one of which,
thirty feet high, now stands on Monte Pincio.   An
obelisk twenty-two feet high, of Syenite granite, was
brought by Mr. Banks from Philæ to England, and now
stands in front of Kingston Lacy Hall, Wimborne.

Among obelisks of obscure origin is one of sandstone
nine feet high at Alnwick; two in the town of Florence,
and one sixty feet high, in the city of Arles, made of grey
granite from the neighbouring quarries of Mont Esterel.
The total number of existing obelisks is fifty-five.   Of
these thirty-three are standing, and twenty-two lie
prostrate on the ground or are buried amid rubbish.
Of those standing, twenty-seven are made of Syenite
granite.

CHAPTER III.

THE LARGEST STONES OF THE WORLD.

IT is interesting to compare the obelisk on the Embankment with the other large stones of the world ; stones, of course, that have been quarried and utilized by man. Of this kind, the largest in England are the blocks at Stonehenge. The biggest weighs about eighteen tons, and is raised up twenty-five feet, resting, as it does, on two upright stones. These were probably used for religious purposes, and their bulk has excited in all ages the wonder of this nation.

The London Obelisk weighs one hundred and eighty-six tons, and therefore is about ten times the weight of Stonehenge's largest block. It is therefore by far the largest stone in England. The obelisk was moreover hoary with the age of fifteen centuries when the trilithons of Stonehenge were set up, and therefore its colossal mass and antiquity may well fill our minds with amazement and veneration.

The individual stones of the pyramids, large though they are, and wonderful as specimens of masonry, are nevertheless small compared with the giant race of the obelisks.

The writer, when inspecting the outer wall of the Temple Hill at Jerusalem, measured a magnificent polished stone, and found it to be twenty-six feet long, six feet high, and seven feet wide. It is composed of solid limestone, and weighs about ninety tons. This stone occupies a position in the wall one hundred and ten feet above the rock on which rest the foundation stones, and arouses wonder at the masonic and engineering skill of the workmen of King Solomon and Herod the Great. This block, however, is only half the weight of Cleopatra's Needle, and even this obelisk falls far short in bulk of many of Egypt's gigantic granite stones.

At Alexandria, Pompey's Pillar is still to be seen. It is a beautifully finished column of red granite, standing outside the walls of the old town. Its total length is about one hundred feet, and its girth round the base twenty-eight feet. The shaft is made of one stone, and probably weighs about three hundred tons.

Even more gigantic than Pompey's Pillar is a colossal block found on the plain of Memphis. Next to Thebes, in Upper Egypt, Memphis was the most important city of ancient Egypt. Here lived the Pharaohs while the Israelites sojourned in the land, and within sight of this sacred city were reared the mammoth pyramids. "As the hills stand round about Jerusalem, so stand the pyramids round about Memphis."

A few grassy mounds are the only vestiges of the once mighty city ; and in the midst of a forest of palm trees is an excavation dug in the ground, in which lies a huge granite block, exposed to view by the encompassing *débris* being cleared away. This huge block is a gigantic

Colossal Statue of Rameses II., at Memphis.

statue lying face downwards. It is well carved, the face
wears a placid countenance, and its size is immense. The
nose is longer than an umbrella, the head is about ten feet
long, and the whole body is in due proportion; so that
the colossal monolith (for it is one stone) probably weighs
about four hundred tons.

In the day of Memphis' glory a great temple, dedicated to Ptah, was one of the marvels of the proud city.
"Noph" (Memphis) "shall be waste and desolate," saith
Jeremiah; a prediction literally fulfilled. Of the great
temple not a vestige remains; but Herodotus says that
in front of the great gateway of the temple, Rameses II.,
called by the Greeks Sesostris, erected a colossal statue
of himself. The colossal statue has fallen from its lofty
position, and now lies prostrate, buried amid the ruins of
the city, as already described. On the belt of the colossus
is the cartouche of Rameses II. The fist and big toe of
this monster figure are in the British Museum. In the
Piazza of St. John Lateran, at Rome, the tall obelisk
towers heavenwards like a lofty spire, adorning that
square. Originally it was one hundred and ten feet long,
and therefore the longest monolith ever quarried. It was
also the heaviest, weighing, as it does, about four hundred
and fifty tons, and therefore considerably more than
twice the weight of the London obelisk.

As the sphinx is closely associated with the obelisk,
and as Thothmes is four times represented by a sphinx
on the London Obelisk, and as, moreover, two huge
sphinxes have lately been placed on the Thames Em-

bankment, one on each side of the Needle, it may not be out of place to say a few words respecting this sculptured figure. An Egyptian sphinx has the body of a lion couchant with the head of a man. The sphinxes seem for the most part to have been set up in the avenues leading to the temples. It is thought by Egyptologists that the lion's body is a symbol of power, the human head is a symbol of intellect. The whole figure was typical of kingly royalty, and set forth the power and wisdom of the Egyptian monarch.

In ancient Egypt, sphinxes might be numbered by thousands, but the gigantic figure known by pre-eminence as "*The Sphinx*," stands on the edge of the rocky platform on which are built the pyramids of Ghizeh. When in Egypt, the writer examined this colossal figure, and found that it is carved out of the summit of the native rock, from which indeed it has never been separated. On mounting its back he found by measurement that the body is over one hundred feet long. The head is thirty feet in length, and fourteen feet in width, and rears itself above the sandy waste. The face is much mutilated, and the body almost hidden by the drifting sand of the desert. It is known that the tremendous paws project fifty feet, enclosing a considerable space, in the centre of which formerly stood a sacrificial altar for religious purposes. On a cartouche in front of the figure is the name of Thothmes IV.; but as Khufu, commonly called Cheops, the builder of the great pyramid, is stated to have repaired the Sphinx, it appears that the colossus had an existence before the pyramids were built. This being so, "The Sphinx" is not only the most colossal, but at the same time the oldest known idol of the human race.

One of the most appreciative of travellers thus describes the impression made upon him by this hoary sculpture :—

" After all that we have seen of colossal statues, there was something stupendous in the sight of that enormous head—its vast projecting wig, its great ears, its open eyes, the red colour still visible on its cheek ; the immense proportion of the whole lower part of its face. Yet what must it have been when on its head there was the royal helmet of Egypt ; on its chin the royal beard ; when the stone pavement by which men approached the pyramids ran up between its paws ; when immediately under its breast an altar stood, from which the smoke went up into the gigantic nostrils of that nose, now vanished from the face, never to be conceived again! All this is known with certainty from the remains that actually exist deep under the sand on which you stand, as you look up from a distance into the broken but still expressive features. And for what purpose was this sphinx of sphinxes called into being, as much greater than all other sphinxes as the pyramids are greater than all other temples or tombs? If, as is likely, he lay couched at the entrance, now deep in ·sand, of the vast approach to the second, that is, the central pyramid, so as to form an essential part of this immense group ; still more, if, as seems possible, there was once intended to be a brother sphinx on the northern side as on the southern side of the approach, its situation and significance were worthy of its grandeur.   And if further the sphinx was the giant representative of royalty, then it fitly guards the greatest of royal sepulchres, and with its half human, half animal form, is the best welcome and the best farewell to the history and religion of Egypt."— Stanley's *Sinai and Palestine*, p. lviii.

Standing amid the sand of the silent desert, gazing upon the placid features so sadly mutilated by the devastations of ages, the colossal figure seemed to awake from sleep, and speak thus to the writer :—

" Traveller, you have wandered far from your peaceful home in sea-girt England, and you long to gaze upon the crumbling glories of the ages that are passed.   You have come to see the marvels of Egypt—the land which in the march of civilization took the lead of all the nations of antiquity.   Here as strangers and pilgrims sojourned the patriarchs Abraham and Jacob.   This was the adopted land of the princely Joseph, the home of Moses, and the abode of Israel's oppressed race.   I remember them well, for from the land of Goshen they all came to see me, and as they gazed at my countenance they were filled with amazement at my greatness and my beauty.   You have heard of the colossal grandeur of Babylon and Nineveh, and the might of Babylonia and Assyria.   You know by fame of the glories of Greece, and perhaps you have seen on the Athenian Acropolis those chaste temples of Pericles, beautiful even in their decay.   You have visited the ruins of ancient Rome, and contemplated with wonder the ruined palace of the Cæsars, Trajan's column, Constantine's arches, Caracalla's baths, and the fallen grandeur of the Forum.

"Traveller, long before the foundation of Rome and Athens; yea, long before the ancient empires of Assyria and Babylonia rose from the dim twilight, I stood here on this rocky platform, and was even old when Romulus and Cecrops, when Ninus and Asshur, were in their infancy.   You have just visited the pyramids of Cheops and Cephren; you marvel at their greatness, and revere their antiquity.   Over these mighty sepulchres I have kept guard for forty centuries, and here I stood amid the solitude of the desert ages before the stones were quarried for these vast tombs.   Thus have I seen the rise, growth, and decay of all the great kingdoms of the earth.   From me then learn this lesson: 'grander than any temple is the temple of the human body, and more sacred than any shrine is the hidden sanctuary of the human soul. Happiness abideth not in noisy fame and vast dominion, but, like a perennial stream, happiness gladdens the soul of him who fears the Most High, and loves his fellow men.   Be content, therefore, with thy lot, and strive earnestly to discharge the daily duties of thine office.'

"This world, with all its glittering splendours, the kings of the earth, and the nobles of the people, are all mortal, even as thou art.   The tombs which now surround me, where reposes the dust of departed greatness, proclaim that you are fast hastening to the destiny they have reached. Change and decay, which you now see on every side, is written on the brow of the monarch as much as on the fading flower of the field. Only the 'Most High' changeth not. He remaineth the same from generation to generation. Trust in Him with all thine heart, serve Him with all thy soul, and all will be well with thee, even for evermore."

CHAPTER IV.

THE LONDON OBELISK.

SEVEN hundred miles up the Nile. beyond Cairo, on the frontiers of Nubia, is the town of Syene or Assouan. In the neighbourhood are the renowned quarries of red granite called Syenite or Syenitic stone. The place is under the tropic of Cancer, and was the spot fixed upon through which the ancients drew the chief parallel of latitude, and therefore Syene was an important place in the early days of astronomy. The sun was of course vertical to Syene at the summer solstice, and a deep well existed there in which the reflection of the sun was seen at noon on midsummer-day.

About fifteen centuries before the Christian era, in the reign of Thothmes III., by royal command, the London Obelisk, together with its companion column, was quarried at Syene, and thence in a huge raft was floated down the Nile to the sacred city of Heliopolis, a distance of seven hundred miles. Heliopolis, called in the Bible On, and by the ancient Egyptians An, was a city of temples dedicated to the worship of the sun. It is a place of high antiquity, and was one of the towns of the land of Goshen. Probably the patriarch Abraham sought refuge here when driven by famine out of the land of Canaan. Heliopolis is inseparably connected with the life of Joseph, who, after being sold to Potiphar as a slave, and after suffering imprisonment on a false accusation, was by Pharaoh promoted to great honour, and by royal command received "to wife Asenath, the daughter of Poti-pherah, priest of On" (Gen. xli. 45). Heliopolis was probably the scene of the affecting meeting of Joseph and his aged father Jacob. The place was not only a sacred city, but it was also a celebrated seat of learning, and the chief university of the ancient world. "Moses was learned in all the wisdom of the Egyptians," and his wisdom he acquired in the sacred college of Heliopolis. Pythagoras and Plato, and many other Greek philosophers, were students at this Egyptian seat of learning.

On arriving at Heliopolis, the two obelisks now called Cleopatra's Needles were set up in front of the great temple of the sun. There they stood for fourteen centuries, during which period many dynasties reigned and passed away; Greek dominion in Egypt rose and flourished, until the Ptolemies were vanquished by the Cæsars, and Egypt became a province of imperial Rome.

Possibly Jacob and Joseph, certainly Moses and Aaron, Pythagoras and Plato, have gazed upon these two obelisks; and therefore the English nation should look at the hoary monolith on the Thames Embankment with feelings of profound veneration.

In the eighth year of Augustus Cæsar, 23 B.C., the Roman Emperor caused the two obelisks to be taken down and transported from Heliopolis to Alexandria,

CLEOPATRA'S NEEDLE, AT ALEXANDRIA.

The prostrate one is now on the Embankment, the other in New York.

there to adorn the Cæsarium, or Palace of the Cæsars. "This palace stood by the side of the harbour of Alexandria, and was surrounded by a sacred grove. It was ornamented with porticoes, and fitted up with libraries, paintings and statues, and was the most lofty building in the city. In front of this palace Augustus set up the two ancient obelisks which had been made by Thothmes III., and carved by Rameses II., and which, like the other monuments of the Theban kings, have outlived all the temples and palaces of their Greek and Roman successors." The obelisks were set up in front of the Cæsarium seven years after the death of Cleopatra, the beautiful though profligate queen of Egypt, and the last of the race of the Ptolemies. Cleopatra may have designed the Cæsarium, and made suggestions for the decoration of the palace. The setting up of the two venerable obelisks may have been part of her plan ; but although the monoliths are called Cleopatra's Needles, it is certain that Cleopatra had nothing to do with their transfer from Heliopolis to Alexandria.

Cleopatra, it appears, was much beloved by her subjects; and it is not improbable that they associated her name with the two obelisks as a means of perpetuating the affectionate regard for her memory.

The exact date of their erection at Alexandria was found out by the recent discovery of an inscription, engraved in Greek and Latin, on a bronze support of one of the obelisks. The inscription in Latin reads thus : "Anno viii Caesaris, Barbarus praefectus Ægypte posuit.

Architectore Pontio." " In the eighth year of Cæsar, Barbarus, prefect of Egypt, erected this, Pontius being the architect."

The figure of an obelisk is often used as a hieroglyph, and is generally represented standing on a low base. The bronze supports reproduced at the bottom of the London Obelisk never appear in the hieroglyphic representations, and were probably an invention of the Ptolemies or the Cæsars.

For about fifteen centuries the two obelisks stood in their new position at Alexandria. The grand palace of the Cæsars, yielding to the ravages of Time's resistless hand, has for many ages disappeared. The gradual encroachment of the sea upon the land continued through the course of many centuries, and ultimately, by the restless action of the waves, the obelisk which now graces our metropolis became undermined, and about 300 years ago the colossal stone fell prostrate on the ground, leaving only its companion to mark the spot where once stood the magnificent palace of the imperial Cæsars.

In 1798 Napoleon Buonaparte, with forty thousand French troops, landed on the coast of Egypt, and soon conquered the country. Admiral Nelson destroyed the French fleet in Aboukir Bay; and at a decisive battle fought within sight of Cleopatra's Needle in 1801, Sir Ralph Abercrombie completely defeated the French army, and rescued Egypt from their dominion. Our soldiers and sailors, wishful to have a trophy of their Nile victories, conceived the idea of bringing the prostrate column to England. The troops cheerfully subscribed part of their pay, and set to work to move the obelisk. After considerable exertions they moved it only a few feet, and the undertaking, not meeting with the approval of the commanders of the army and navy, was unfortunately abandoned. Part of the pedestal was, however, uncovered and raised, and a small space being chiselled out of the surface, a brass plate was inserted, on which was engraved a short account of the British victories.

George IV., on his accession to the throne in 1820, received as a gift the prostrate obelisk from Mehemet Ali, then ruler of Egypt. The nation looked forward with hope to its speedy arrival in England, but for some reason the valuable present was not accepted. In 1831 Mehemet Ali not only renewed his offer to King William IV., but promised also to ship the monolith free of charge. The compliment, however, was declined with thanks. In 1849 the Government announced in the House of Commons their desire to transport it to London, but as the opposition urged "that the obelisk was too much defaced to be worth removal," the proposal was not carried out. In 1851, the year rendered memorable by the Great Exhibition in Hyde Park, the question was again broached in the House, but the estimated outlay of £7,000 for transport was deemed too large a grant from the public purse. In 1853 the Sydenham Palace Company, desirous of having the obelisk in their Egyptian court, expressed their wish to set it up in the transept of the Palace, and offered to pay all expenses.

The consent of the Government was asked for its removal, but the design fell through, because, as was urged, national property could only be lent, not given to a private company.

Great diversity of opinion existed about that time respecting its value, even among the leading Egyptologists; for in 1858 that enthusiastic Egyptian scholar, Sir Gardner Wilkinson, referring to Mehemet Ali's generous offer, said:—"The project has been wisely abandoned, and cooler deliberation has pronounced that from its mutilated state and the obliteration of many of the hieroglyphics by exposure to the sea air, it is unworthy the expense of removal."

In 1867 the Khedive disposed of the ground on which the prostrate Needle lay to a Greek merchant, who insisted on its removal from his property. The Khedive appealed to England to take possession of it, otherwise our title to the monument must be given up, as it was rapidly being buried amid the sand. The appeal, however, produced no effect, and it became evident to those antiquaries interested in the treasures of ancient Egypt, that if ever the obelisk was to be rescued from the rubbish in which it lay buried, and transported to the shores of England, the undertaking would not be carried out by our Government, but by private munificence.

The owner of the ground on which it lay actually entertained the idea of breaking it up for building material, and it was only saved from destruction by the timely intervention of General Alexander, who for ten successive years pleaded incessantly with the owner of the ground, with learned societies and with the English Government, for the preservation and removal of the monument. The indefatigable General went to Egypt to visit the spot in 1875. He found the prostrate obelisk hidden from view and buried in the sand ; but through the assistance of Mr. Wyman Dixon, C.E., it was uncovered and examined.

On returning to England, the General represented the state of the case to his friend Professor Erasmus Wilson, and the question of transport was discussed by these two gentlemen together with Mr. John Dixon, C.E. The latter after due consideration gave the estimated cost at £10,000, whereupon Professor Wilson, inspired with the ardent wish of rescuing the precious relic from oblivion, signed a bond for £10,000, and agreed to pay this sum to Mr. Dixon, on the obelisk being set up in London. The Board of Works offered a site on the Thames Embankment, and Mr. Dixon set to work *con amore* to carry out the contract.

Early in July, 1877, he arrived at Alexandria, and soon unearthed the buried monolith, which he was delighted to find in much better condition than had been generally represented. With considerable labour it was encased in an iron watertight cylinder about one hundred feet long, which with its precious treasure was set afloat. The *Olga* steam tug was employed to tow it, and on the 21st September, 1877, steamed out of the harbour of Alexandria *en route* for England. The voyage for twenty days was a prosperous one, but on the 14th October, when in the Bay of Biscay, a storm arose, and the pontoon cylinder was raised on end. At midnight it was thought to be foundering, and to save the crew its

CLEOPATRA'S NEEDLE, ON THE THAMES EMBANKMENT.

connection with the *Olga* was cut off. The captain, thinking that the Needle had gone to the bottom of the sea, sailed for England, where the sorrowful tidings soon spread of the loss of the anxiously expected monument. To the great delight of the nation, it was discovered that the pontoon, instead of sinking, had floated about for sixty hours on the surface of the waters, and having been picked up by the steamer *Fitzmaurice*, had been towed to Vigo, on the coast of Spain. After a few weeks' delay it was brought to England, and set up in its present position on the Thames Embankment.

The London Needle is about seventy feet long, and from the base, which measures about eight feet, it gradually tapers upwards to the width of five feet, when it contracts into a pointed pyramid seven feet high. Set up in its original position at Heliopolis about fifteen centuries before the Christian era, this venerable monument of a remote antiquity is nearly thirty-five centuries old.

" Such is the British Obelisk, unique, grand, and symbolical, which devotion reared upward to the sun ere many empires of the West had emerged from obscurity. It was ancient at the foundation of the city of Rome, and even old when the Greek empire was in its cradle. Its history is lost in the clouds of mythology long before the rise of the Roman power. To Solomon's Egyptian bride the Needle must have been an ancestral monument ; to Pythagoras and Solon a record of a traditional past antecedent to all historical recollection. In the college near the obelisk, Moses, the meekest of all men, learned the wisdom of the Egyptians. When, after the terrible last plague, the mixed multitude of the Israelites were driven forth from Egypt, the light of the pillar of fire threw the shadow of the obelisk across the path of the fugitives. Centuries later, when the wrecked empire of Judæa was dispersed by the king of Babylon, it was again in the precincts of the obelisk of On that the·

exiled people of the Lord took shelter. Upon how many scenes has that monolith looked!" Amid the changes of many dynasties and the fall of mighty empires it is still preserved to posterity, and now rises in our midst—the most venerable and the most valuable relic of the infancy of the world.

"This British Obelisk," says Dean Stanley, "will be a lasting memorial of those lessons which are taught by the Good Samaritan. What does it tell us as it stands, a solitary heathen stranger, amidst the monuments of our English Christian greatness—near to the statues of our statesmen, under the shadow of our Legislature, and within sight of the precincts of our Abbey? It speaks to us of the wisdom and splendour which was the parent of all past civilization, the wisdom whereby Moses made himself learned in all the learning of the Egyptians for the deliverance and education of Israel—whence the earliest Grecian philosophers and the earliest Christian Fathers derived the insight which enabled them to look into the deep things alike of Paganism and Christianity. It tells us—so often as we look at its strange form and venerable characters—that 'the Light which lighteneth every man' shone also on those who raised it as an emblem of the beneficial rays of the sunlight of the world. It tells us that as true goodness was possible in the outcast Samaritan, so true wisdom was possible even in the hard and superstitious Egyptians, even in that dim twilight of the human race, before the first dawn of the Hebrew Law or of the Christian Gospel."

CHAPTER V.

How the Hieroglyphic Language was Recovered.

On the triumph of Christianity, the idolatrous religion of the ancient Egyptians was regarded with pious abhorrence, and so in course of time the hieroglyphics became neglected and forgotten. Thus for fifteen centuries the hieroglyphic inscriptions that cover tombs, temples, and obelisks were regarded as unmeaning characters. Thousands of travellers traversed the land of Egypt, and yet they never took the trouble to copy with accuracy a single line of an inscription. The monuments of Egypt received a little attention about the middle of the eighteenth century, and vague notions of the nature of hieroglyphs were entertained by Winckelman, Visconti, and others. Most of their suggestions are of little value; and it was not until the publication of the description of ancient Egypt by the first scientific expedition under Napoleon that the world regained a glimpse of the true nature of the long-forgotten hieroglyphs.

In 1798 M. Boussard discovered near Rosetta, situated at one of the mouths of the Nile, a large polished stone of black granite, known as "The Rosetta Stone." This celebrated monument it appears was set up in the

temple of Tum at Heliopolis about 200 B.C., in honour
of Ptolemy V., according to a solemn decree of the
united priesthood in synod at Memphis.   On its discovery, the stone was presented to the French Institute
at Cairo ; but on the capture of Alexandria by the
British in 1801, and the consequent defeat of the French
troops, the Rosetta Stone came into the possession
of the English general, and was presented by him to
King George III.   The king in turn presented the

THE ROSETTA STONE.

precious relic to the nation, and the stone is now in
safe custody in the British Museum.

The Rosetta Stone has opened the sealed book of
hieroglyphics, and enabled the learned to understand
the long-forgotten monumental inscriptions.   On the
stone is a trigrammatical inscription, that is, an inscription thrice repeated in three different characters ; the

first in pure hieroglyphs, the second in Demotic, and the third in Greek.   The French savants made the first attempt at deciphering it; but they were quickly followed by German, Italian, Swedish, and English scholars. Groups of characters on the stone were observed amid the hieroglyphs to correspond to the words, Alexander, Alexandria, Ptolemy, king, etc., in the Greek inscription Many of the opinions expressed were very conflicting, and most of them were ingenious conjectures.   A real advance was made in the study when, in 1818, Dr. Young, a London physician, announced that many of the characters in the group that stood for Ptolemy must have a phonetic value, somewhat after the manner of our own alphabet.   M. Champollion, a young French savant, deeply interested in Egyptology, availed himself of Dr. Young's discovery, and pursued the study with ardent perseverance.

In 1822 another inscribed monument was found at Philæ, in Upper Egypt, which rendered substantial help to such Egyptologists as were eagerly striving to unravel the mystery of the hieroglyphs.   It was a small obelisk with a Greek inscription at the base, which inscription turned out to be a translation of the hieroglyphs on the obelisk.   Champollion found on the obelisk a group of hieroglyphs which stood for the Greek name Kleopatra ; and by carefully comparing this group with a group on the Rosetta Stone that stood for Ptolemy, he was able to announce that Dr. Young's teaching was correct, inasmuch as many of the hieroglyphs in the roval names are alphabetic phonetics, that is, each represents a letter sound, as in the case of our own alphabet.

Champollion further announced that the phonetic hieroglyph stood for the initial letter of the name of the object represented. Thus, in the name Kleopatra, the first hieroglyph is a knee, called in Coptic *kne*, and this sign stands for the letter *k*, the first letter in Kleopatra. The second hieroglyph is a lion couchant, and stands for *l*, because that letter is the first in *labu*, the Egyptian name of lion. Further, by comparing the names of Ptolemy and Kleopatra with that of Alexander, Champollion discovered the value of fifteen phonetic hieroglyphs. In the pursuit of his studies he also found out the existence of homophones, that is, characters having the same sound; and that phonetics were mixed up in every inscription with ideographs and representations.

In 1828, the French Government sent Champollion as conductor of a scientific expedition to Egypt. He translated the inscriptions with marvellous facility, and seemed at once to give life to the hitherto mute hieroglyphs. On a wall of a temple at Karnak, amidst the prisoners of King Shishak, he found the name "Kingdom of Judah." It will be remembered that the Bible states that "In the fifth year of King Rehoboam, Shishak, King of Egypt, came up against Jerusalem: and he took away the treasures of the house of the Lord, and the treasures of the king's house" (1 Kings xiv, 25, 26). The discovery, therefore, of the name "Kingdom of Judah" in hieroglyphs in connection with Shishak excited much interest in the Christian world, corroborating as it did the Biblical narrative.

In 1830 Champollion returned from Egypt laden with the fruits of his researches; and by his indefatigable genius he worked out the grand problem of the deciphering and interpretation of hieroglyphic inscriptions.

Since that time the study of Egyptology has been pursued by Rosellini, Bunsen, De Rouge, Mariette, Lenormant, Brugsch, Lepsius, Birch, Poole, etc. The number of hieroglyphs at present are about a thousand. A century ago there existed no hope of recovering the extinct language of the ancient Egyptians; but by the continued labours of genius, the darkness of fifteen centuries has been dispelled, and the endless inscriptions covering obelisks, temples and tombs, proclaim in a wondrous manner the story of Egypt's ancient greatness.

Dr. Brugsch has written a long and elaborate history of Egypt, derived entirely from "ancient and authentic sources;" that is, from the inscriptions on the walls of temples, on obelisks, etc., and from papyri. The work has been translated into English, and published with the title, "Egypt under the Pharaohs." The student also has only to turn to the article "Hieroglyphics" in Vol. XI. of the ninth edition of the "Encyclopædia Britannica," to see what progress has been made recently in this direction.

But notwithstanding all this, the language of the hieroglyphs is not yet by any means perfectly understood and Egyptian grammar still presents many knotty problems that await solution. Rapid strides are daily being made in the study of Egyptology ; and it may be hoped that the time is not far distant when the student will read hieroglyphic inscriptions with the same facility that the classic student reads a page of Greek and Latin.

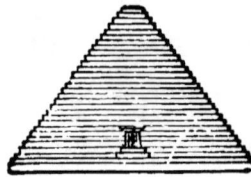

CHAPTER VI.

THE INTERPRETATION OF HIEROGLYPHICS.

HIEROGLYPHS or hieroglyphics, literally "sacred sculptures," is the term applied to those written characters by means of which the ancient Egyptians expressed their thoughts. Hieroglyphs are usually pictures of external objects, such as the sun, moon, stars, plants, animals, man, the members of man's body, and various other objects.

They may be arranged in four classes.

First. *Representational, iconographic,* or *mimic* hieroglyphs, in which case each hieroglyph is a picture of the object referred to. Thus, the sun's disk means the sun; a crescent the moon; a whip means a whip; an eye, an eye. Such hieroglyphs form picture-writing, and may be called *iconographs*, or representations.

Secondly. *Symbolical, tropical,* or *ideographic* hieroglyphs, in which case the hieroglyph was not designed to stand for the object represented, but for some quality or attribute suggested by the object. Thus, heaven and a star meant night; a leg in a trap, deceit; incense, adoration; a bee, Lower Egypt; the heart, love; an eye with a tear, grief; a beetle, immortality; a crook, protection. Such hieroglyphs are called *ideographs*, and are perhaps the most difficult to interpret, inasmuch as they stand for abstract ideas. Ideographic writing was carried to great perfection, the signs for ideas became fixed, and each ideograph had a stereotyped signification.

Thirdly. *Enigmatic* hieroglyphs include all those wherein one object stands for some other object. Thus, a hawk stands for a solar deity ; the bird ibis, for the god Thoth ; a seated figure with a curved beard, for a god.

Fourthly. *Phonetic* hieroglyphs, wherein each hieroglyph represents a sound, and is therefore called a phonetic. Each phonetic at first probably stood for a syllable, in which case it might be called a syllabic sign. Thus, a chessboard represents the sound *men;* a hoe, *mer ;* a triple twig, *mes;* a bowl, *neb;* a beetle, *khep ;* a bee, *kheb;* a star, *seb.*

It appears that when phonetic hieroglyphs were first formed, the spoken language was for the most part made up of monosyllabic words, and that the names given to animals were imitations of the sounds made by such animals ; thus, *ab* means lamb; *ba,* goat ; *au,* cow ; *mau,* lion ; *su,* goose; *ui,* a chicken ; *bak,* a hawk; *mu,* an owl ; *khep,* a beetle ; *kheb,* a bee, etc.

It is easy to see how the figure of any such animal would stand for the name of the animal. According to Dr. Birch, the original monosyllabic words usually began with a consonant, and the vowel sound between the two consonants of a syllable was an indifferent matter, because the name of an object was variously pronounced in different parts; thus a guitar, which is an ideograph meaning goodness, might be pronounced *nefer* or *nofer;* a papyrus roll, which stood for oblation, was called *hetep* or *hotep.*

Most phonetics remained as syllabic signs, but many of them in course of time lost part of the sound embodied in the syllable, and stood for a letter sound only. Thus, the picture of a lion, which at first stood for the whole sound *labo,* the Egyptian name of lion, in course of time stood only for *l,* the initial sound of the word; an owl first stood for *mu,* then for *m;* a water-jug stood first for *nen,* then for *n,* its initial letter.

Phonetics which represent letters only and not syllables may be called *alphabetic* signs, in contradistinction to *syllabic* signs.

Plutarch asserts that the ancient Egyptians had an alphabet of twenty-five letters, and although in later epochs of Egyptian history there existed at least two hundred alphabetic signs, yet at a congress of Egyptologists held in London in 1874, it was agreed that the ancient recognized alphabet consisted of twenty-five letters. These were as follows:—An eagle stood for *a;* a reed, *à;* an arm, *ā;* leg, *l;* horned serpent, *f;* mæander, *h;* pair of parallel diagonals, *i;* knotted cord, *ḥ;* double reed, *ī;* bowl, *k;* throne or stand, *ḳ;* lion couchant, *l;* owl, *m;* zigzag or waterline, *n;* square or window shutter, *p;* angle or knee, *q;* mouth, *r;* chair or crochet, *s;* inundated garden or pool, *sh;* semicircle, *ṭ;* lasso or sugar-tongs-shaped noose, *th;* hand, *ṭ;* snake, *t';* chicken, *ui;* sieve, *kh.*

	a	Eagle	....	....	'Aa
	à	Reed		....	.... Au
	ā	Arm	....	....	... Aa
4	b	Leg		....	.... Bu
5	f	Cerastes Serpent	....		Fi
6	h	Mæander		....	.... Ha
7	h	Knotted Cord		....	.... Hi
8	i	Pair of parallel diagonals			
9	ī	Double Reed		....	.... iu
10	k	Bowl	....	....	.... Kâ
11	ḳ	Throne (stand)		....	... Qa
12	l	Lion couchant		....	.... Lu or Ru
13	m	Owl	....		Mu
14	n	Zigzag or Water Line		.	Na
15	p	Square or Window-blind (shutter)			Pu
16	q	Angle (Knee)			Qa
17	r	Mouth	....	....	... Ru, Lu
18	s	Chair or Crochet	....		Sen or Set
19	s	Inundated (?) Garden (Pool)			Shi
20	t	Semicircle		....	... Tu
21	θ	Lasso (sugar-tongs-shaped) Noose			Ti
22	ṭ	Hand	....	....	.... Ti
23	t'	Snake	....	....	.... —
24		Chick	....	....	ui
25	χ	Sieve	....	....	.... Khi

About 600 B.C., during the XXVIth dynasty, many hieroglyphs, about a hundred in number, which previously were used as ideographs only, had assigned to them a phonetic value, and became henceforth alphabetic signs as well as ideographs.   In consequence of this innovation, in the last ages of the Egyptian monarchy, we find many hieroglyphs having the same phonetic value.   Such hieroglyphs are called homophones, and they are sometimes very numerous; for instance, as many as twenty hieroglyphs had each the value of *a*, and *h* was represented by at least thirty homophones. In spite of the great number of homophones, the Egyptians usually spelled their words by consonants only, after the manner of the ancient Hebrews; thus, *hk* stood for *hek*, a ruler; *htp* for *hotep*, an offering; *km* for *kam*, Egypt; *ms* for *mes*, born of.

The Egyptians began at an early age to use syllabic signs for proper names.   Osiris was a well-known name; and as *os* in their spoken language meant a throne, and *iri*, an eye, a small picture of a throne followed by that of an eye, stood for *Osiri*, the name of their god.

An ideograph was often preceded and followed by two phonetic signs, which respectively represented the initial and final sound of the name of the ideograph. Thus a chessboard was an ideograph, and stood for a gift, and sometimes a building.   It was called *men*, and sometimes the chessboard is preceded by an owl, the phonetic sign of *m*, and followed by a zigzag line, the phonetic sign of *n*.   Such complementary hieroglyphs are intended primarily to show with greater precision the pronunciation of *men*, and they are known by the name of complements.

Phonetic hieroglyphs are often followed by a representation or ideograph of the object referred to. Such explanatory representations and ideographs are called determinatives, because they help to determine the precise value of the preceding hieroglyph.

They were rendered necessary on the monuments from the fact that the Egyptians had few vowel sounds; thus *nib* meant an ibis; *nebi*, a plough; *neb*, a lord; but each word was represented by the consonantal signs *n-b;* and consequently it was necessary to put after *n-b* a determinative sign of an ibis or a plough, to show which of the two was meant.

From the earliest to the latest ages of the Egyptian monarchy, all kinds of hieroglyphs are used in the same inscription, iconographs, ideographs, and phonetics are mingled together; and if it were not for the judicious use of complements and determinatives, it would often be impossible to interpret the inscriptions.

The hieroglyphs constitute the most ancient mode of writing known to mankind. They were used, as the name hieroglyphs, that is, "sacred sculptures," implies, almost exclusively for sacred purposes, as may be proved from the fact that the numerous inscriptions found on temples, tombs and obelisks relate to the gods and the religious duties of man. Hence the Egyptians called their written language *neter tu*, which means "sacred words." The hieroglyphs at present known are about a thousand, but further discoveries may augment their number.   On the monuments they are arranged with artistic care, either in horizontal lines or in vertical columns, with all the animals and symbols facing one way, either to the right hand or the left.

The hieroglyphs on obelisks and other granite monuments are sculptured with a precision and delicacy that excite the admiration of the nineteenth century.   In tombs and on papyri the hieroglyphs are painted sometimes with many colours, while on obelisks and on the walls of temples they are generally carved in a peculiar style of cutting known as *cavo relievo*, that is, raised relief sunk below the surface.   The beautiful artistic effect of the coloured hieroglyphs as seen on some of the tombs is as much superior to our mode of writing as the flowing robes of the Orientals as compared with the dress of the Franks.   The spoken language of the Egyptians was Semitic, but it had little in common with the Hebrew, for Joseph conversed with his brothers by means of an interpreter.

Hieroglyphic inscriptions are found in the earliest tombs.   The cartouche of Khufu, or Cheops, a king of the IVth dynasty, was found on a block of the great pyramid ; and as hieroglyphic inscriptions were used until the age of Caracalla, a Roman emperor of the third century, it follows that hieroglyphs were used as a mode of writing for about three thousand years.

The Egyptians had two modes of cursive writing.

The *hieratic*, used by the priests and employed for sacred writings only. The hieratic characters, which are really abbreviated forms of hieroglyphics, bear the same relation to the hieroglyphs that our handwriting does to the printed text. Another mode of cursive writing used by the people and employed in law, literature, and secular matters, is known as *demotic* or *enchorial*. The characters in demotic are derived from the hieratic, but appear in a simpler form, and phonetics largely prevail over ideographs.

To any students who wish to pursue the absorbing study of hieroglyphics, the following works are recommended:—"Introduction to the Study of Hieroglyphics," by Dr. Samuel Birch; "Egyptian Texts," by the same author, and "Egyptian Grammar," by P. Le Page Renouf. The two latter works are published in Bagster's series of Archaic Classics. Wilkinson's "Ancient Egyptians," and Cooper's "Egyptian Obelisks," are instructive volumes. The author obtained much help from the works of Champollion, Rosellini, Sharpe, Lepsius, and from Vol. II. of "Records of the Past."

CHAPTER VII.

THOTHMES III.

THOTHMES III. is generally regarded as the greatest
of the kings of Egypt—the Alexander the Great of
Egyptian history. The name Thothmes means "child
of Thoth," and was a common name among the ancient
Egyptians. On the pyramidion of the obelisk he is
represented by a sphinx presenting gifts of water
and wine to Tum, the setting sun, a solar deity worshipped at Heliopolis. On the hieroglyphic paintings
at Karnak, the fact of the heliacal rising of Sothis,
the dog-star, is stated to have taken place during this
reign, from which it appears that Thothmes III.
occupied the throne of Egypt about 1450 B.C. This is
one of the few dates of Egyptian chronology that can
be authenticated.

Thothmes III. belonged to the XVIIIth dynasty,
which included some of the greatest of Egyptian
monarchs. Among the kings of this dynasty were
four that bore the name of Thothmes, and four the
name of Amenophis, which means "peace of Amen."
The monarchs of this dynasty were Thebans.

The father of Thothmes III. was a great warrior. He

conquered the Canaanitish nations of Palestine, took
Nineveh from the Rutennu, the confederate tribes of
Syria, laid waste Mesopotamia, and introduced the war-
chariots and horses into the army of Egypt.

Thothmes III., however, was even a greater warrior
than his father; and during his long reign Egypt reached
the climax of her greatness.   His predecessors of the
XVIIIth dynasty had extended the dominions of Egypt
far into Asia and the interior of Africa.   He was a king
of great capacity and a warrior of considerable courage.
The records of his campaigns are for the most part
preserved on a sandstone wall surrounding the great
temple of Karnak, built by Thothmes III. in honour
of Amen-Ra.   From these hieroglyphic inscriptions it
appears that Thothmes' first great campaign was made
in the twenty-second year of his reign, when an expedition was made into the land of Taneter, that is, Palestine.
A full account of his marches and victories is given,
together with a list of one hundred and nineteen conquered towns.

This monarch lived before the time of Joshua, and
therefore the records of his conquests present us with
the ancient Canaanite nomenclature of places in Palestine
between the times of the patriarchs and the conquest of
the land by the Israelites under Joshua.   Thothmes set
out with his army from Tanis, that is, Zoan ; and after
taking Gaza, he proceeded, by way of the plain of Sharon,
to the more northern parts of Palestine.   At the battle
of Megiddo he overthrew the confederated troops of native

princes; and in consequence of this signal victory the whole of Palestine was subdued. Crossing the Jordan near the Sea of Galilee, Thothmes pursued his march to Damascus, which he took by the sword; and then returning homewards by the Judean hills and the south country of Palestine, he returned to Egypt laden with the spoils of victory.

In the thirtieth year of his reign Thothmes lead an expedition against the Rutennu, the people of Northern Syria. In this campaign he attacked and captured Kadesh, a strong fortress in the valley of Orontes, and the capital town of the Rutennu. The king pushed his conquests into Mesopotamia, and occupied the strong fortress of Carchemish, on the banks of the Euphrates. He then led his conquering troops northwards to the sources of the Tigris and the Euphrates, so that the kings of Damascus, Nineveh, and Assur became his vassals, and paid tribute to Egypt.

Punt or Arabia was also subdued, and in Africa his conquests extended to Cush or Ethiopia. His fleet of ships sailed triumphantly over the waters of the Black Sea. Thus Thothmes ruled over lands extending from the mountains of Caucasus to the shores of the Indian Ocean, and from the Libyan Desert to the great river Tigris.

" Besides distinguishing himself as a warrior and as a record writer, Thothmes III. was one of the greatest of Egyptian builders and patrons of art. The great temple of Ammon at Thebes was the special object of his fostering care, and he began his career of builder and restorer by repairing the damages which his sister Hatasu had inflicted on that glorious edifice to gratify her dislike of her brother Thothmes II., and her father Thothmes I. Statues of Thothmes I. and his father Amenophis, which Hatasu had thrown down, were re-erected by Thothmes III. before the southern propylæa of the temple in the first year of his independent reign. The central sanctuary which Usertesen I. had built in common stone, was next replaced by the present granite edifice, under the directions of the young prince, who then proceeded to build in rear of the old temple a magnificent hall or pillared chamber of dimensions previously unknown in Egypt. This edifice was an oblong square one hundred and forty-three feet long by fifty-five feet wide, or nearly half as large again as the nave of Canterbury Cathedral. The whole of this apartment was roofed in with slabs of solid stone ; two rows of circular pillars thirty feet in height supported the central part, dividing it into three avenues, while on each side of the pillars was a row of square piers, still further extending the width of the chamber, and breaking it up into five long vistas. In connection with this noble hall, on three sides of it, north, east, and south, Thothmes erected further chambers and corridors, one of the former situated towards the south containing the ' Great Table of Karnak.'

"Other erections of this distinguished monarch are the enclosure of the temple of the Sun at Heliopolis, and the obelisks belonging to the same building, which the irony of fate has now removed to Rome, England, and America; the temple of Ptah at Thebes; the small temple at Medinet Abou; a temple at Kneph, adorned with obelisks, at Elephantine, and a series of temples and monuments at Ombos, Esneh, Abydos, Coptos, Denderah, Eileithyia, Hermonthis and Memphis in Egypt; and at Amada, Corte, Talmis, Pselus, Semneh, and Koummeh in Nubia. Large remains still exist in the Koummeh and Semneh temples, where Thothmes worships Totun, the Nubian Kneph, in conjunction with Usertesen III., his own ancestor. There are also extensive ruins of his great buildings at Denderah, Ombos, and Napata. Altogether Thothmes III. is pronounced to have 'left more monuments than any other Pharaoh, excepting Rameses II.,' and though occasionally showing himself as a builder somewhat capricious and whimsical, yet still on the whole to have worked in 'a pure style,' and proved that he was 'not deficient in good taste.'

" There is reason to believe that the great constructions of this mighty monarch were, in part at least, the product of forced labours. Doubtless his eleven thousand captives were for the most part held in slavery, and compelled to employ their energies in helping towards the accomplishment of those grand works which his active mind was continually engaged in devising. We find among the monuments of his time a representation of the mode in which the services of these foreign bondsmen were made

E

to subserve the glory of the Pharaoh who had carried them away captive. Some are seen kneading and cutting up the clay; others bear them water from a neighbouring pool; others again, with the assistance of a wooden mould, shape the clay into bricks, which are then taken and placed in long rows to dry; finally, when the bricks are sufficiently hard, the highest class of labourers proceed to build them into walls. All the work is performed under the eyes of taskmasters, armed with sticks, who address the labourers with the words: 'The stick is in my hand, be not idle.' Over the whole is an inscription which says: 'Here are to be seen the prisoners which have been carried away as living captives in very great numbers; they work at the building with active fingers; their overseers are in sight; they insist with vehemence' (on the others working), 'obeying the orders of the great skilled lord' (i.e., the head architect), 'who prescribes to them the works, and gives directions to the masters; they are rewarded with wine and all kinds of good dishes; they perform their service with a mind full of love for the king; they build for Thothmes Ra-men-khepr a Holy of Holies for the gods. May it be rewarded to him through a range of many years."*

"In person Thothmes III. does not appear to have been very remarkable. His countenance was thoroughly Egyptian, but not characterised by any strong individuality. The long, well-shaped, but somewhat delicate nose, almost in a line with the forehead, gives a slightly

* Rawlinson's "History of Ancient Egypt," Vol. II., pp. 240–243.

feminine appearance to the face, which is generally represented as beardless and moderately plump. The eye,
prominent, and larger than that of the ordinary Egyptian,
has a pensive but resolute expression, and is suggestive
of mental force. The mouth is somewhat too full for

COLOSSAL HEAD OF THOTHMES III.

beauty, but is resolute, like the eye, and less sensual
than that of most Egyptians. There is an appearance
of weakness about the chin, which is short, and retreats
slightly, thus helping to give the entire countenance a
womanish look. Altogether, the face has less of strength

E 2

and determination than we should have expected, but is not wholly without indications of some of those qualities."*

Thothmes III. died after a long and prosperous reign of fifty-four years, and when he was probably about sixty years old, his father having died when he was only an infant.

* Rawlinson's " History of Ancient Egypt," Vol. II., p. 253.

CHAPTER VIII.

THE HIEROGLYPHICS OF THOTHMES III.

———o———

Translation of the First Side.

"The Horus, powerful Bull, crowned in Uas, King of Upper and Lower Egypt, 'Ra-men-Kheper.' He has made as it were monuments to his father Haremakhu; he has set up two great obelisks capped with gold at the first festival of Triakonteris. According to his wish he has done it, Son of the Sun, Thothmes, beloved of Haremakhu, ever-living."

" Horus, powerful Bull, crowned in Uas."

HAWK (bak) *Horus.* Horus is a solar deity, and represented the rising sun, or the sun in the horizon. Horus is here represented by a hawk, surmounted by the double crown of Egypt called PSCHENT. The hawk flew higher than any other bird of Egypt, and therefore became the usual emblem of any solar deity, just as the eagle, from its lofty soaring, is an emblem of sublimity, and therefore an emblem of

St. John. The double crown named PSCHENT is composed of a conical -hat called HET, the crown and emblem of Upper Egypt, and the TESHER, or red crown, the emblem of Lower Egypt. The wearer of the double crown was supposed to exercise authority over the two Egypts. The oblong form upon the top of which the sacred hawk, the symbol of Horus, stands, is thought by some to be a representation of the standard of the monarch. Dr. Birch thinks it is the ground plan of a palace, and the avenue and approaches to the palace.

BULL (Mnevis). The *Mnevis* was the name of the black bull, or sacred ox of Heliopolis. It was regarded as an avatar or incarnation of a solar deity. On the London Obelisk Mnevis appears twelve times on the palatial titles, and twice on the lateral columns of Rameses II.

ARM WITH STICK (khu) *powerful,* is the common symbol of power. In the Bible also an arm stands for power. "The Lord brought us forth out of Egypt with a mighty hand and with an outstretched arm" (Deut. xxvi. 8). There are twelve palatial titles on the obelisk, three on each face, and in eleven cases occurs the arm holding a stick in its hand. In each case this hieroglyph may be rendered by the word *powerful.* The same hieroglyph appears several times in both the central and lateral columns.

CROWN (kha) *crowned,* because placed on the head at the time of coronation. This hieroglyph is thought by some to be a part of a dress.

OWL (em) *in,* is a preposition.

SCEPTRE (Uas) *Western Thebes.* The sceptre here depicted is that carried in the left hand of Theban kings. It is composed of three parts, the top is the head of a greyhound, the shaft is the long stalk of some reed, perhaps that of the papyrus or lotus, while the curved bo'tom represents the claws of the crocodile, an animal common in Upper Egypt in ancient times. This sceptre, called KAKUFA, was often represented by an ostrich feather, the common symbol of truth, and stands for *Uas,* the name of that part of Thebes which stood on the western bank of the Nile. The sceptre as an ideograph means power, in the same manner as the sceptre carried by our monarch on state occasions is a badge of authority.

Thus the palatial title may be rendered, "The powerful bull, crowned in Western Thebes."

Above the cartouche will be noticed a group of four

hieroglyphs, namely, a *reed*, *bee*, and two *semicircles*. This group is usually placed above the cartouche containing the prenomen or sacred name of the king, and the four are descriptive of the authority exercised by the monarch.   They may be thus explained :—

REED (**su**) is the symbol of Upper Egypt, where reeds of this kind were probably common, especially by the banks of the Nile.   A flower or plant is often used as the emblem of a nation.

In ancient times the vine was the emblem of the king of Judah, and on the same principle the reed was the emblem of Upper Egypt.   The semicircle below is called *tu*, and here stands for king.   The two hieroglyphs together are called SUTEN, and may be rendered "king of Upper Egypt."

BEE (**kheb**) is the emblem of Lower Egypt.

The four hieroglyphs are called SUTEN-KHEB, and mean "king of Upper and Lower Egypt."

The bee was an insect that received great attention among the ancient Egyptians.   They were kept in hives which resembled our own, and when flowers were nòt numerous, the owners of bees often carried their hives in boats to various spots on the banks of the Nile where many flowers were blooming.   The wild bees frequented the sunny banks and made their habitations in the clefts of the rocks.   Moses says that God made His people to "suck honey out of the rock," and the Psalmist repeats the same idea, when he says, "with honey out of the rock should I have satisfied thee."

Below this group of hieroglyphs stands what is called the cartouche of Thothmes III.   The word was first used by Champollion, and signifies a scroll or label, or escutcheon on which the name of a king is inscribed. The oval form of the cartouche was probably taken from the scarabeus or sacred beetle, an emblem of the resurrection and immortality ; and thus the very framework on which the king inscribed his name spoke of the eternity of a future state. The form, however, may be from a plate of armour. The cartouche is somewhat analogous to a heraldic shield bearing a coat of arms, and its object was probably to give prominence to the king's name, just as an aureole in Christian art gives prominence to the figure it encloses.

The three hieroglyphs charged in this cartouche make up the divine name of Thothmes, and consist of a solar disk, chessboard, and beetle. Each monarch had two names, respectively called prenomen, or divine name, somewhat analogous to our Christian name, and the nomen, corresponding to our surname. The prenomen is called the divine name, because it contains the name of the god from whom the king claims his descent, and often the deities also by whom he is beloved, and with whom he claims relationship. The king not only claimed descent from the gods, but he was accounted by his subjects as a representation of the deity.

The title of Pharaoh applied to their kings is derived from Phaa or Ra, the midday sun, and the notion was taught that kingly power was derived from the supreme solar deity. The divine right of kings was thus an article of faith among the ancient Egyptians. He was the head of their religious system, defender of the faith ;

and in all matters, ecclesiastical as well as civil, the king was supreme. He was consequently instructed in the mysteries of the gods, the services of the temples, and the duties of the priesthood. The Theban kings claimed relationship with Amen, the supreme god of Thebes ; and most kings also claimed Ra, the supreme solar deity, worshipped at Heliopolis, as their grand ancestor.

SUN's DISK (aten) was the emblem of Ra, who was said to have in per-fection all the attributes possessed by inferior deities. He was all in all ; from him came, and to him return. the souls of men.

Ra or Phra was, properly speaking, the mid-day sun ; and as the sun shines with greatest power and brightness at mid-day, the attributes of majesty and authority were intimately associated with this deity. Amen-Ra, the god of Thebes, was supposed to possess the attributes of Amen and Ra.

The ATEN was originally circular, and thus in shape resembled the sun's disk, but in many inscriptions the shape is oval, or that of an oblate-spheroid, considerably flattened at top and bottom.

CHESSBOARD (men) is by many thought to be a battlemented wall, but it is probably a chessboard ; for at Thebes a picture represents Rameses III, playing a game at chess, or some kindred game. What appears to be a battlement is really the chessmen on the board.

MEN, as part of the divine name of Thothmes, may be the shortened form of Amen, the supreme god of Thebes, just as Tum is the shortened form of Atum. Ptah was the supreme god of Memphis, and Ra the supreme god of Heliopolis. Amen literally means " the concealed one," and was the name applied to the sun after it had sunk below the horizon. He was reputed to be the oldest and most venerable of deities, called the " dweller in eternity," and the source of light and life.

Before the creation he dwelt alone in the lower world, but on his saying "come," the sun appeared, and drove away the darkness of night. Sometimes he is called Amen-Ra, and his principal temple was at Thebes. He is generally represented by the figure of a man with his face concealed under the head of a horned ram. The figure is coloured blue, the sacred colour of the source of life.

SACRED BEETLE (kheper) usually called *scarabeus* or *scarabee*. It was thought that the beetle hid its eggs in the sand, where they remained until the young beetles broke forth to life. Thus the scarabeus became the symbol of the resurrection and a future life.

According to Cooper, the sacred beetle was in the habit of laying its eggs in a ball of clay, which it kept rolling until the eggs were vivified by the heat of the sun. The beetle thus became the emblem of the sun, the vivifier, and was therefore consecrated to Ra, who is on that account called Ra-Kheper.

When dedicated to Ra, the beetle holds the cosmic ball between its front legs. Sometimes it is an emblem of the world, and is then consecrated to Ptah, the creator of heaven and earth.

The divine name, or prenomen, of Thothmes is thus *Ra-Men-Kheper*, frequently read *Men-Khepera-Ra*, and is made up of three hieroglyphs, which stand for Ra, Amen, and Ptah, the supreme gods respectively worshipped at Heliopolis, Thebes, and Memphis. From these three great deities Thothmes thus claims his descent.

The cartouche with the divine name of Thothmes occurs four times on the obelisk, once on each side at the top of the central column of hieroglyphs. The sacred beetle occurs in two other places in the central columns of Thothmes, but never appears in the eight lateral columns of Rameses.

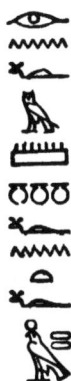

" He has made as it were
monuments to
his father
Haremakhu."

EYE (ar) *made*. As a verb *ar* signifies to make.

ZIGZAG (en) *has*. After verbs the zigzag means *has*, and is therefore a sign of perfect.

HORNED SNAKE (ef) *he*. The usual personal pronoun.

OWL (mu) *as it were.*

CHESSBOARD (men) *monument.*

VASE (nu). The vase represents an *ampulla* or bottle. The three vases in this place are used as a determinative to *men*, monument ; and being three in number, indicate plurality, making MEN into MENU, monuments.

HORNED SNAKE (ef) *his*. This figure is often called cerastes. Standing by itself it usually stands for the possessive pronoun *his*.

ZIGZAG (en) *to*. Used here as a preposition.

SEMICIRCLE and CERASTES (tef) *father*. The semicircle is here an alphabetic phonetic, equal to *t*, and with *ef* makes TEF, meaning father.

HAWK (bak) *Horus*. The hawk alone stood for any solar deity. With the solar disk on the head and two ovals by the side, as in the present hieroglyph, it stood for Haremakhu, the sun in the horizon. The two ovals are called KHU, and stand for the eastern and western horizons.

Thothmes III. claims Horus as his father, and it is moreover evident from the above that the obelisk itself is dedicated to the rising sun. The great Sphinx at the pyramids of Ghizeh is also dedicated to Haremakhu, and this may account for the fact that the gigantic figure faces the east, the region of the rising sun.

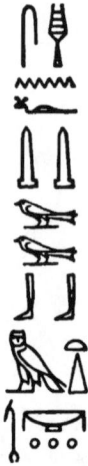

"He has set up
two great obelisks
capped with gold."

THRONE BACK (es). This may be the back of a chair. It is the old hieroglyph for the letter *s*.

REEL (ha) *set up*. This hieroglyph is by some thought to be the leg of a stool.

ZIGZAG (en) *has*.

HORNED SNAKE (ef) *he*.

OBELISK (*tekhen*) is in this place an image or picture of the thing spoken of, namely obelisk. This hieroglyph is therefore an iconograph, or representation. Two obelisks are here depicted, to indicate that two were set up. According to Cooper the obelisk was an emblem of the sun—the clearest symbol of supreme deity. The Egyptian name was TEKHEN, a word signifying mystery, and it was regarded among the initiated as the esoteric symbol of light and life. The obelisk was consequently dedicated to Horus, the god of the rising sun, while the pyramid, the house of the dead, was dedicated to Tum, or Atum, the god of the setting sun. Hence obelisks are found only on the east bank of the Nile, while pyramids are built on the west side, by the edge of the silent desert.

SWALLOW (ur) *great*. The swallow is an emblem of greatness, and therefore may be called an ideograph, or symbolic hieroglyph.

Two swallows are here depicted, because there are two obelisks, and the dual form extends to the adjective.

TWO LEGS (bu) *capped*. There are two legs, to express duality, and thus agree with the preceding substantive, two obelisks. A human leg is the original alphabetic sign for letter *b*. The letter *u* is a plural termination.

SEMICIRCLE (ta) *the.*   Under the right leg is a semicircle, which is here
the feminine article to agree with the little triangular hieroglyph below.

PYRAMIDION.   The summit of the obelisk, known as the pyramidion, from
its resemblance to a small pyramid, is here represented by a small
triangle.   This hieroglyph represents the top or cap of the obelisk, and
is a determinative to *capped.*

OWL (mu) *with.*   Owl, as a preposition, has the same meaning as the
prepositions *with, from, by*—the usual signs of the ablative case.

BOWL (neb) *gold.*   Under this crater or bowl will be noticed three small
dots, probably designed to represent grains of the metal intended.

SCEPTRE (user) is here used as a determinative of metal; and some
Egyptologists think that when it accompanies the bowl called NEB, the
metal referred to is not gold but copper.

Among the hieroglyphs on the London Obelisk may
be found many ideographs or pictures of outward objects,
each of which stands for an attribute or abstract idea.
Thus arm stands for power, interior of a hall for festivity,
lizard for multitude, beetle for immortality, sceptre for
power, crook for authority, Anubis staff for plenty, vulture
for queenly royalty, asp for kingly royalty, ostrich feather
for truth, ankh or crux ansata for life, weight for equality,
adze for approval, pike for power, horn for opposition, the
bird called bennu for lustre, pyramous loaf for giving,
hatchet called neter for god, lion's head for victory,
swallow for greatness.

In addition to the obelisk, the other iconographs or
picture representations found on the London Obelisk
are the sun, moon, star, heaven, pole, throne, abode,
altar, tree.

From this hieroglyphic sentence we learn that the
pyramidion of each obelisk was covered or capped with
some metal, probably copper.   This was done to protect

the monument from lightning and rain. Cooper draws attention to the fact that obelisks were capped with metals, and pyramids were covered with polished stones. The pyramidia of Hatasu's obelisks at Karnak were covered with gold. The venerable obelisk still standing at Heliopolis had a cap of bronze, which remained until the Middle Ages, and was seen by an Arabian physician about A.D. 1300.

The avarice of greed and the rapacity of war have long since stripped every obelisk of its metal covering.

"At the first festival

of the Triakonteris."

DISK (**aten**) *time.* The solar disk is usually a symbol of Ra, but as the sun is the measurer of times and seasons, the disk sometimes stands for time, as it does here.

　　The hieroglyphs following are defaced. Some think one hieroglyph is a cerastes, but Dr. Birch says the group probably consisted of a harpoon and three vertical lines—a common sign of plurality. Thus the preceding sentence would be "at time the first," that is, "at the first time."

OWL (**mu**) *in.* Here a preposition governing *time.*

PALACE (**seḥ**) *Festival of the Triakonteris.* This hieroglyph with three compartments probably represents the interior of a palace. It is the usual symbol for a festival. With two small thrones inside, as seen here, the hieroglyph probably represents the interior of a palace ; and is the ideograph for the festival called triakonteris, because celebrated every thirty years. This cyclical festival was celebrated with great festivity. The space of time between two successive feasts was called a triakontennial period.   The thrones which distinguish the triakonteris from an ordinary festival indicates also the royal character of this great feast.

HALL (seh) is the usual hieroglyph for an ordinary festival, and represents the interior of a hall.   It consists of two compartments.   The pole in the centre supporting the roof is here a carved post.   *Seh* is here used as a determinative to the preceding hieroglyph.   The symbol for festival here stands on a large semicircle, with an inscribed diamond-shaped aperture.   This semicircle with the diamond-shaped aperture is called HEB, and often appears alone as the hieroglyph for *festival*.

Thothmes III. reigned fifty-four years, and therefore witnessed the beginning of two triakontennial periods. Probably he set up the two obelisks at the first triakonteris that happened during his reign.

The hieroglyphs following seem to be zigzag, line, semicircle, zigzag, hoe, mouth, mouth, cerastes, semicircle, two arms united, line, eye, zigzag, cerastes.   These are defaced somewhat on the obelisk, and therefore doubtfully copied in the transcript.   Dr. Birch translates them : "according to his wish he has done it."   The student should notice that the hieroglyphs hoe and mouth together mean *wish*.

Eye (ar) here means *done;* and zigzag *has*, the usual sign of perfect.

The nomen is the family name or surname of the monarch.   It may be made up of iconographs, ideographs, syllabic signs, and alphabetic phonetics ; or the name may consist of a combination of all these.   If it be composed of the first three, then the nomen corresponds to what in heraldry is called a rebus.   The name of Thothmes is made up of the well-known sacred bird called *ibis*, and the triple twig called *mes*.

"Son of the Sun,
Thothmes."

GOOSE (sa) *son*. The goose was a common article of food in Egypt, and as hieroglyphs for the most part are representations of common objects, we find the goose repeatedly figured on the inscriptions. Sometimes it stands for *Seb*, the father of the gods, the *Saturn* of classic mythology.

SOLAR DISK (aten) *the sun*. It stands for Ra, the sun-god. The goose and disk mean "son of the sun," and almost invariably precede the nomen of the king, because kings were thought to be lineal descendants of the supreme solar deity,

IBIS. A common bird in Egypt, resembling the crane, phœnix, and bennu. It was sacred to, and an emblem of, Thoth, the god of letters, who is usually depicted with an ibis head. As Thoth represented both the visible and concealed moon, he was fitly represented by the sacred bird ibis, which on account of its mingled black and white feathers, was an effective emblem of both the dark and illumined side of the moon. The ibis alone on a standard, as depicted on the obelisk, stood for Thoth, the first syllable of the word Thothmes.

TRIPLE TWIG (mes) means *born*, and is a symbol of birth. Thus *ibis* and *mes* together form the rebus Thothmes, which name thus means, "born of Thoth."

In this particular cartouche will be noticed a small scarabeus or beetle, which is an emblem of existence and immortality, and probably indicates the self-existent nature and immortality of Thothmes; but this part of the obelisk is much defaced, and what follows is well nigh obliterated.

In ancient times kings and great persons were frequently named after the god they worshipped ; thus
among the Egyptians, Rameses from Ra, Amen-hotep
from Amen, Seti from Set, etc.   Similarly in Scripture
we find Joshua, Jeremiah, Jesus, derived from Jehovah ;
Jerubbaal, Ethbaal, Jezebel, Belshazzar, and many others,
from Baal or Bel, the sun-god ; Elijah, Elisha, Elias,
Elishama, etc., from El or Eloah, the true God.   The
same mode of deriving names from deities prevailed
more or less among all ancient nations.   On this principle Thothmes, the mighty Egyptian monarch, was
named after the god Thoth.

What follows on this side of the obelisk is well nigh
obliterated, but the hieroglyphs were probably the same
as those following the cartouche of Thothmes at the
bottom of the central column on the second and fourth
sides of the obelisk, and therefore would mean, "Beloved
of Haremakhu, ever living."

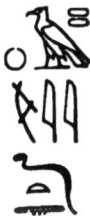

"Beloved of Haremakhu,
ever living."

HAWK (bak), as has been already explained, is the emblem of any solar
deity, but surmounted by the *aten* or solar disk, and accompanied
by two ovals called *khu*, which indicate the two horizons, in the
east and west parts of the sky, the hawk, as here, stands for Horus,
or Haremakhu, the sun in the horizon.

The hoe, called **mer** or **tore**, is equal to the phonetic *m*, and was one of
the commonest implements used in agriculture.   It is sometimes spoken
of as a hand-plough, or pick or spade, and probably it answered all

F

these purposes. In shape it somewhat resembled our capital letter A, as it consisted of two lines tied together about the centre with a twisted rope. One limb was of uniform thickness, and generally straight, and formed the head ; while the other, curved inwards, and sometimes of considerable width, formed the handle. The hoe stands here for the phonetic sound of *m*, the first letter of the word **mai**, which means *beloved*.

Two Reeds. One reed is equal to *a*, the double reed equals phonetic *i*, and is generally a plural sign. Here the double reed is an intensive, so that the hoe and double reeds spell *mai*, which means " much beloved."

These hieroglyphs, taken in the order in which they ought to be translated into English, consist of a hoe, two reeds, a hawk, two ovals, and a solar disk.

The last group of hieroglyphs consists of a long serpent, a semicircle, and a straight line. The long serpent is equal to the phonetic *t*, or *th*, or *g*. The semicircle, which represents the upper grindstone for bruising corn, equals phonetic *t*. It is often called a muller or millstone. The straight line is a phonetic equal to *ta*. The three hieroglyphs therefore form the word *getta* or *tetta*, a term which means everlasting.

Getta appears as the last group of hieroglyphs at the bottom of the central column on the third and fourth sides. They were probably at first at the end of the central column on the first and second sides also, although they have been obliterated on the two latter faces.

CHAPTER IX.

THE HIEROGLYPHICS OF THOTHMES III.

———o———

Translation of the Second Side.

" Horus, the powerful Bull, crowned by Truth, Lord of Upper and Lower Egypt, Ra-men-Kheper. The Lord of the Gods has multiplied Festivals to him upon the great Persea Tree within the Temple of the Phœnix ; he is known as his son—a divine person, his limbs issuing in all places according to his wish. Son of the Sun, Thothmes, of Holy An, beloved of Haremakhu."

" Horus, the powerful bull,
crowned by Truth,
lord of
Upper and Lower Egypt,
Ra-men-Kheper."

SEATED FIGURE (**Ma**) *goddess of Truth.* She was called Thmei or Ma, and was generally represented by a seated female, holding in one hand the ankh, the symbol of life, and on her head an ostrich feather. The ostrich feather alone is also the symbol of truth or justice, because of the equal length of the feathers. In courts of justice the chief judge wore a figure of Thmei suspended from his neck by a golden chain.

F 2

Thmei or Ma is always represented as present at the dreadful balance in the hall of justice, where each soul was weighed against the symbol of divine truth.

The above is the same as face one, the only new idea being that of *Truth*, mentioned in the palatial title.

"The lord of the gods has multiplied Festivals to him."

LIZARD (**as**) *multiplied*. *As* is the usual verb to multiply. With the zigzag line under the sign of the perfect, the two hieroglyphs mean *has multiplied*.

BACK OF CHAIR (**s**) phonetic hieroglyph. Is here the consonantal complement of *as*, the preceding hieroglyph.

ZIGZAG (**en**) *to*. A preposition here.

CERASTES (**ef**) *him*. Personal pronoun.

BASKET (**neb**) *lord*. This hieroglyph might be thought to be a basin, but in painted hieroglyphs it appears as a wicker basket.

THREE HATCHETS (**neteru**) *gods*. A hatchet or battle-axe was called neter, and was the usual symbol for a god. Plurality is often indicated by a hieroglyph being repeated three times. The letter *u* is a plural termination; thus *neter* is god, *neteru* gods.

PALACE (**seh**) *festival*.

HALL (**seh**) *festival*. Here used as a determinative to the preceding.

Every syllabic sign possesses an inherent vowel sound, or an inherent consonant sound, or both. The vowel sign is often placed before, and the consonant sign after the syllabic sign. Such alphabetic hieroglyphs are called complements, and are very frequently used in the inscriptions.

" Upon the great Persea Tree within the Temple of the Phœnix."

HUMAN HEAD (Her) *upon,*
 The vertical line preceding is the masculine article. The defaced signs on the left were probably three short vertical lines, to indicate the plurality of festivals.

POOL (shi). Here a phonetic united with succeeding hieroglyph.

HAND (t) alphabetic phonetic. The two spell *shit,* the name of *persea,* a beautiful tree abounding in ancient Egypt, bearing pear-shaped fruit.

TREE (persea) *tree.* A determinative to the preceding hieroglyphs. The tree here referred to may have been situated at Heliopolis; and it is worthy of notice that in a picture at Thebes, the god Tum appears in the act of writing the name of Thothmes on the fruit of the persea.

PERSON ON THRONE (sep) *great.* The throne is a common symbol for greatness.

CHAIR BACK (s) alphabetic phonetic. Here an initial complement to *sep.*

OWL (em)   } The two form *emkhen,* the preposition
DECAPITATE FIGURE (khen) } *within.*

SEMICIRCLE (tu) *the.* Feminine article.

OPEN SQUARE (ha) *house.* The figure probably represents the ground plan of an ancient house.

LARGE SQUARE (ha) *temple.* This square is not open, but it encloses a smaller square in one corner, and thus resembles a stamped envelope. The god or sacred bird that dwells in this temple is depicted within the square. On the third face of the obelisk, right lateral column, the goddess Athor or Hathor—literally the abode of Horus, thus implying that she was Horus' mother—is represented by a large square, enclosing a hawk, the emblem of Horus. Within the square hieroglyph now under consideration will be noticed the figure of a bird somewhat defaced, probably the crane or phœnix. The square itself is perhaps the ground plan of a temple, or adytum of a temple. Thus the sentence means, " within the house, the temple of the phœnix." Cooper thinks the bird depicted is the *bennu,* the sacred bird of Heliopolis, and that the temple of the bennu, called *habennu,* is the great temple of the sun at Heliopolis.

"He is known as his son,
a divine person.
His limbs issuing
in all places,
according to his wish."

MOUTH (ru)
CIRCLE (aten)   } The two, *ru-aten,* equal *known.*
GOOSE (sa) *son.*
CERASTES (ef) *he.*
CHICK (u) *is.*
HATCHET (neter) *divine.*
HUMAN FIGURE *person.*

Thothmes, in virtue of his royalty, styles himself a " divine person."

TWISTED CORD (hi) *limbs*. The three dots represent fragments of his
   body, and form a determinative of limbs.

HOUSE (p) ⎫
MOUTH (r) ⎭ The two form *per, issuing*.

OWL (em) *in*.

MÆANDER (ha) *place*.

BASKET (neb) *all*.

MOUTH (er) *according to*.

POOL (mer) *wish*.

MOUTH (er) *his*.

Then follows, "son of the sun, Thothmes of An," etc.,
the same hieroglyphs as those already explained at the
lower part of the first column. The only new hieroglyph
is the *pylon*, rendered *An* in the cartouche. It may be
explained as follows :—

PYLON (**An**) *Heliopolis*. The sacred city of the sun must have been a
   city of obelisks, temples, and pylons, or colossal gateways. The
   latter must have formed a conspicuous feature of the place, inasmuch
   as the massive masonry of the gateways would tower high above the
   other buildings. This being so, it is not surprising that a pylon with
   a flagstaff should be the usual symbol for Heliopolis.

The hieroglyphs following the cartouche mean, " Beloved of Haremakhu," etc., and have already been
explained.

It ought to be observed that on three sides of the
obelisk Thothmes' columns of hieroglyphs ended alike,
namely : face one, now almost obliterated in this part ;
face two, still distinct ; and face four, more complete in
its termination than any other side.

CHAPTER X.

THE HIEROGLYPHICS OF THOTHMES III.

———o———

Translation of the Third Side.

"Horus, powerful Bull, beloved of Ra, King of Upper and Lower Egypt, Ra-men-Kheper. His father Tum has set up for him a great name, with increase of royalty, in the precincts of Heliopolis, giving him the throne of Seb, the dignity of Kheper, Son of the Sun, Thothmes, the Holy, the Just, beloved of the Bennu of An, ever-living."

The first part of the inscription, namely, "Horus, powerful bull, beloved of Ra, king of Upper and Lower Egypt, Ra-men-Kheper," is the same as in the first and second side, the only new idea occurring in the lower part of the palatial title, namely, "beloved of Ra."

HAND PLOUGH (**mer**) *beloved.*

FIGURE (**Ra**) *sun-god.* The seated figure has a hawk's head, surmounted by the aten or solar disk. Ra being the supreme solar deity, the "beloved of Ra" was one of the favourite epithets of the king.

" His father Tum
set up for him
a great name,
with increase of
royalty."

CHESSBOARD (men) *set up.*

ZIGZAG (en) *has.* After zigzag appears a thick line, which Dr. Birch thinks to be a papyrus roll, the usual sign of possession.

SEMICIRCLE (t) with cerastes (*ef*) make up (*tef*) *father.*

SEMICIRCLE (t) phonetic consonantal complement of *t* in *Tum.*

SLEDGE (tm) *Tum.* The setting sun, worshipped at Heliopolis, probably same as Atum. The god Tum appears on the four sides of the pyramidion, and some therefore think that the obelisk stood with its companion in front of the temple of Tum at Heliopolis.

MOUTH (ru) *for.*

ZIGZAG (n)
CERASTES (ef) } The two form (*nef*) *him.*

SWALLOW (ur) *great.* This is the usual hieroglyph for greatness.

CARTOUCHE (khen) *name.* The cartouche is usually the oval form in which the king inscribed his name. Here it stands for *name.*

OWL (em) *with.* The owl has generally the force of the ablative case.

TWISTED CORD (uah) *increase.* The top of this hieroglyph resembles papyrus flower, and ought therefore to be distinguished from the simple twisted cord.

REED (su) *royalty.*

" In the precincts
of Heliopolis,
giving him the
throne of Seb,
the dignity of
· Kepher."

OWL (**em**) *m*. Complement to *am*, preceding.

CROSS (**am**) *in*.

SEMICIRCLE (**ta**) the.

OBLONG (**hen**) *precincts*. The usual hieroglyph for temple.

PYLON (**An**) *Heliopolis*.

CIRCLE with CROSS (**nu**) determinative of a city.

MOUTH (**r**) }
ARM (**a**) } The two phonetics form *ra, giving*.

SEMICIRCLE (**ta**) *the*.

CERASTES (**ef**) *him*.

THRONE (**kher**) *throne*.

GOOSE (**s**) } The two phonetics form *sb* or *Seb*, name of a god. Seb was
LEG (**b**) } the Chronos of the Greeks, the Saturn of the Latins.

HORNS ON A POLE (**aa**) *dignity*. On the horns is a coiled rope.

ZIGZAG (**en**) *of*.

BEETLE (**khep**) *Kheper*. The scarabeus or sacred beetle, dedicated to Ra and Ptah.

The remaining hieroglyphs of this · column have

already been explained (*see* p. 80), except the two small hieroglyphs beside the nomen Thothmes, and the termination of the column.

MUSICAL INSTRUMENT (**nefer**) *holy*. This instrument resembles a heart surmounted by a cross. Some think it represents a guitar, and from the purifying effects of music, became the symbol for goodness or holiness.

OSTRICH FEATHER (**shu**) *true*. The usual symbol of truth. The nomen therefore in this case may be rendered, "Thothmes, the holy, the true."

BENNU **bennu**) sacred bird of An. This *bennu* is usually depicted with two long feathers on the back of the head.

"An or Heliopolis."

PYLON or gateway, is a hieroglyph that stands for *An* or *On*, the Greek Heliopolis. Its great antiquity is shown from the fact that the city is referred to in the Book of Genesis under the name of *On*, translated Ὦν in the Septuagint: "And Pharaoh called Joseph's name Zaphnath-paaneah; and he gave him to wife Asenath the daughter of Poti-pherah priest of On . . . . And unto Joseph in the land of Egypt were born Manasseh and Ephraim, which Asenath the daughter of Poti-pherah priest of On bare unto him."

Heliopolis was by the ancient Egyptians named Benbena, "the house of pyramidia;" but as no pyramids proper ever existed at On, the monuments alluded to are either pylons, that is, gateways of temples, or obelisks.

CHAPTER XI.

THE HIEROGLYPHICS OF THOTHMES III.

———o———

Translation of the Fourth Side.

"Horus, beloved of Osiris, King of Upper and Lower Egypt, Ra-men-Kheper, making offerings, beloved of the gods, supplying the altar of the three Spirits of Heliopolis, with a sound life hundreds of thousands of festivals of thirty years, very many; Son of the Sun, Thothmes, divine Ruler, beloved of Haremakhu, ever-living."

The first part of the inscription, "Horus, beloved of Osiris, king of Upper and Lower Egypt, Ra-men-Kheper," is similar to the other faces, except that the figure of Osiris, the benignant declining sun, occurs.

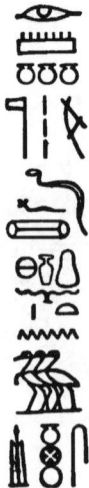

"Making offerings, beloved of the gods, supplying the altar of the three Spirits of Heliopolis."

CHESSBOARD (men) *making.*

THREE VASES (menu) *offerings.* Plurality is indicated by the vase being repeated thrice.

HAND PLOUGH (mer) *beloved.*

HATCHET (neter) *god.* The three vertical lines before the hatchet indicate plurality.

LONG SERPENT (g) phonetic } The two form *gef, supplying.*
HORNED SNAKE (ef) phonetic }

ALTAR, *altar.*

ZIGZAG (nu) *of.*

THREE BIRDS, *three spirits.* These birds represent the bennu, or sacred bird of Heliopolis, supposed to be an incarnation of a solar god. Three are depicted to represent respectively the three solar deities, Horus, Ra, Tum.

PYLON (An) *Heliopolis.*

VASE (n) complement to (*An*).

CIRCLE with CROSS (nu) determinative of city An.

"With a sound life, hundreds of thousands of festivals of thirty years, very many."

OWL (em) *with.*

CROSS (ankh) *life.* This hieroglyph is the usual symbol of life. It is therefore known as the key of life, and from its shape is called *crux ansata,* "handled cross." It ought to be distinguished from the musical instrument called sistrum, which it somewhat resembles.

SCEPTRE (uas) *sound.* The sceptre usually stands for power, but power in life is soundness of health.

LITTLE MAN (hefen) *hundreds of thousands.* This little figure with hands upraised is the usual symbol for an indefinite number, and may be rendered millions, or as above.

PALACE (heb) *festivals.* *See* face one.

SWALLOW (ur) *very.* This symbol generally means great. Here it is an intensive, very.

LIZARD (ast) *many.*

"Making offerings
to their Majesties
at two seasons
of the year, that
he might repose by
means of them."

OFFERING (hotep) *offering.* The three vertical lines indicating plurality may refer both to offering and succeeding hieroglyph.

CONE (hen) *majesty.* We have called this cone, from its likeness to a fir-cone.

TWO CIRCLES (aten) *two seasons.* Each is a solar disk, the ordinary symbol of Ra, but here means season, because seasons depend on the sun.

SHOOT (renpa) *year.* This is a shoot of a palm tree; with one notch it equals year.

The following hieroglyphs are obscure, but the highest authorities say that they probably mean, "that he might repose by means of them;" that is, that Thothmes hoped that repose might be brought to his mind from the fact that he made due offerings to his gods at the two appointed seasons.

CHAPTER XII.

RAMESES II.

THE lateral columns of hieroglyphics on the London Obelisk are the work of Rameses II., who lived about two centuries after Thothmes III., and ascended the throne about 1300 B.C. Rameses II. was the third king of the XIXth dynasty; and for personal exploits, the magnificence of his works, and the length of his reign, he was not surpassed by any of the kings of ancient Egypt, except by Thothmes III.

His grandfather, Rameses I., was the founder of the dynasty. His father, Seti I., is celebrated for his victories over the Rutennu, or Syrians, and over the Shasu, or Arabians, as well as for his public works, especially the great temple he built at Karnak. Rameses II. was, however, a greater warrior than his father. He first conquered Kush, or Ethiopia; then he led an expedition against the Khitæ, or Hittites, whom he completely routed at Kadesh, the ancient capital, a town on the River Orontes, north of Mount Lebanon. In this battle Rameses was placed in the greatest danger; but his personal bravery stood him in good stead, and he kept the Hittites at bay till his soldiers rescued him. He thus commemorates on the monuments his deeds :

"I became like the god Mentu; I hurled the dart with my right hand; I fought with my left hand; I was like Baal in his time before their sight; I had come upon two thousand five hundred pairs of horses; I was in the midst of them; but they were dashed in pieces before my steeds. Not one of them raised his hand to fight; their courage was sunken in their breasts; their limbs gave way; they could not hurl the dart, nor had they strength to thrust the spear. I made them fall into the waters like crocodiles; they tumbled down on their faces one after another. I killed them at my pleasure, so that not one looked back behind him; nor did any turn round. Each fell, and none raised himself up again."*

Rameses fought with and conquered the Amorites, Canaanites, and other tribes of Palestine and Syria. His public works are also very numerous; he dug wells, founded cities, and completed a great wall begun by his father Seti, reaching from Pelusium to Heliopolis, a gigantic structure, designed to keep back the hostile Asiatics, thus reminding one of the Great Wall of China. Pelusium was situated near the present Port Saïd, and the wall must therefore have been about a hundred miles long. In its course it must have passed near the site of Tel-el-Kebir. It is now certain that Rameses built the treasure cities spoken of in Exodus: "Therefore they did set over them taskmasters to afflict them with their burdens. And they built for Pharaoh treasure cities. Pithom and Raamses" (Exod. i. 11). According to

* Brugsch, "History of Egypt," Vol. II., p. 57, 1st ed.

Dr. Birch, Rameses II. was a monarch of whom it was written : "Now there arose up a new king over Egypt who knew not Joseph."

He enlarged On and Tanis, and built temples at Ipsambul, Karnak, Luxor, Abydos, Memphis, etc.

" The most remarkable of the temples erected by Rameses is the building at Thebes, once called the Memnonium, but now commonly known as the Rameseum ; and the extraordinary rock temple of Ipsambul, or Abu-Simbel, the most magnificent speci-men of its class which the world contains.

"The façade is formed by four huge colossi, each seventy feet in height, representing Rameses himself seated on a throne, with the double crown of Egypt upon his head. In the centre, flanked on either side by two of these gigantic figures, is a doorway of the usual Egyptian type, opening into a small vestibule, which communi-cates by a short passage with the main chamber. This is an oblong square, sixty feet long, by forty-five, divided into a nave and two aisles by two rows of square piers with Osirid statues, thirty feet high in front, and orna-mented with painted sculptures over its whole surface. The main chamber leads into an inner shrine, or adytum, supported by four piers with Osirid figures, but other-wise as richly adorned as the outer apartment. Behind the adytum are small rooms for the priests who served in the temple. It is the façade of the work which con-stitutes its main beauty."*

* Rawlinson's "Ancient Egypt," Vol. II., p. 318.

G

"The largest of the rock temples at Ipsambul," says Mr. Fergusson, "is *the finest of its class known to exist anywhere*. Externally the façade is about one hundred

COLOSSAL HEAD OF RAMESES II.

feet in height, and adorned by four of the most magnificent colossi in Egypt, each seventy feet in height, and representing the king, Rameses II., who caused the excavation to be made. It may be because they are more perfect than any other now found in that country, but certainly nothing can exceed their calm majesty and beauty, or be more entirely free from the vulgarity and exaggeration which is generally a characteristic of colossal works of this sort."*

A great king Rameses was, undoubtedly; but he showed no disposition to underrate his greatness. The hieroglyphics on Cleopatra's Needles are written in a vaunting and arrogant strain; and in all the monuments celebrating his deeds the same spirit is present. His character has been well summarized by Canon Rawlinson ·—

"His affection for his son, and for his two principal wives, shows that the disposition of Rameses II. was in some respects amiable; although, upon the whole, his character is one which scarcely commends itself to our approval. Professing in his early years extreme devotion to the memory of his father, he lived to show himself his father's worst enemy, and to aim at obliterating his memory by erasing his name from the monuments on which it occurred, and in many cases substituting his own. Amid a great show of regard for the deities of his country, and for the ordinances of the established worship, he contrived that the chief result of all that he did for religion should be the glorification of himself. Other kings had arrogated to themselves a certain qualified dignity, and after their deaths had sometimes been placed by some of their successors on a par with the

* "History of Architecture," Vol. I., p. 113.

real national gods; but it remained for Rameses to associate himself during his lifetime with such leading deities as Ptah, Ammon, and Horus, and to claim equally with them the religious regards of his subjects. He was also, as already observed, the first to introduce into Egypt the degrading custom of polygamy and the corrupting influence of a harem. Even his bravery, which cannot be denied, loses half its merit by being made the constant subject of boasting; and his magnificence ceases to appear admirable when we think at what a cost it displayed itself. If, with most recent writers upon Egyptian history, we identify him with the 'king who knew not Joseph,' the builder of Pithom and Raamses, the first oppressor of the Israelites, we must add some darker shades to the picture, and look upon him as a cruel and ruthless despot, who did not shrink from inflicting on innocent persons the severest pain and suffering."

CHAPTER XIII.

THE HIEROGLYPHICS OF RAMESES II.

First side.—Right hand.

"Horus, powerful bull, son of Tum, king of Upper and Lower Egypt, Ra-user-ma-sotep-en-Ra, lord of kingly and queenly royalty, guardian of Kham (Egypt), chastiser of foreign lands, son of the sun, Ra-meri-Amen, dragging the foreigners of southern nations to the Great Sea, the foreigners of northern nations to the four poles of heaven, lord of the two countries, Ra-user-ma-sotep-en-Ra, son of the sun, Ra-mes-su-men-Amen, giver of life like the sun."

Most of the above hieroglyphs have already been explained, but the following remarks will enable the reader to understand better this column of hieroglyphs.

Cartouche containing the divine name of Rameses :—

"King of Upper and
Lower Egypt,
Ra-user-ma-sotep-en-Ra."

OVAL (aten) *Ra.* The oval is the solar disk, the usual symbol of the supreme solar deity called Ra.

ANUBIS STAFF (**user**) *abounding in*. This symbol was equal to Latin *dives*, rich, abounding in. The *user*, or Anubis staff, was a rod with a jackal-head on the top. The jackal was the emblem of Anubis, son of Osiris, and brother of Thoth. The god Anubis was the friend and guardian of pure souls. He is therefore frequently depicted by the bed of the dying. After death Anubis was director of funeral rites, and presided over the embalmers of the dead. He was also the conductor of souls to the regions of Amenti, and in the hall of judgment presides over the scales of justice.

FEMALE FIGURE (**ma**) *Ma* or *Thmei*, the goddess of truth. She is generally represented in a sitting posture, holding in her hand the *ankh*, the key of life, an emblem of immortality.

DISK (**aten**) *Ra*, the supreme solar deity.

DRILL OR AUGER (**sotep**) *approved*. *Sotep* means to judge, to approve of. Here it simply means *approved*.

ZIGZAG (**en**) *of*.

The prenomen, or divine name of Rameses, means " The supreme solar god, abounding in truth, approved of Ra."   Thus in his divine nature Rameses claims to be a descendant of Ra, and of the same nature with the god.   This prenomen is repeated twice in each column of hieroglyphs, and as there are eight lateral columns cut by Rameses, it follows that this divine name occurs sixteen times on the obelisk.

" Lord of kingly and
queenly royalty,
guardian of Egypt,
chastiser of
foreign lands."

THE VULTURE (mut) was worn on the diadem of a queen, and was a badge of queenly royalty.

THE SACRED ASP, called *uræus*, was worn on the forehead of a king. It was a symbol of kingly royalty and immortality, and being worn by the king (Βασιλευς), the sacred asp was also called *basilisk*. Rameses, in choosing the epithet " Lord of kingly and queenly royalty," wished perhaps to set forth that he embodied in himself the graces of a queen with the wisdom of a king.

CROCODILE'S TAIL (**Kham**) *Egypt*. *Kham* literally means black, and Egypt in early times was called " the black country," from the black alluvial soil brought down by the Nile. The symbol thought to be a crocodile's tail represents Egypt, because the crocodile abounded in Egypt, and was a characteristic of that country. Even at the present time Egypt is sometimes spoken of as " the land of the crocodile."

TWO STRAIGHT LINES (**tata**) is the usual symbol for the two countries of Egypt. They appear above the second prenomen of this column of hieroglyphs. Each line represents a layer of earth, and is named *ta*. Egypt was a flat country, and on this account the emblem of Egypt was a straight line.

A figure with an undulating surface, called *set*, is the usual emblem of a foreign country. The undulating surface probably indicates the hills and valleys of those foreign lands around Egypt, such as Nubia, Arabia Petra, Canaan, Phœnicia, etc. These countries, in comparison with the flat land of Egypt, were countries of hills and valleys. This hieroglyph for foreign lands occurs in this column immediately above the first nomen.

Cartouche with nomen : " Ra-mes-es Meri-Amen."

FIGURE WITH HAWK'S HEAD is Ra. On his head he wears the *aten*, or solar disk, and in his hand holds the *ankh*, or key of life.

TRIPLE TWIG (mes) is here the syllabic *mes*. This is the usual symbol for *birth* or *born*; thus the monarch in his name *Rameses* claims to be *born of Ra*.

CHAIR BACK (s). The final complement in *mes*.

REED (es) *es*. The final syllable in name Rameses. Some are disposed to render the reed as *su*, and thus make the name Ramessu. With his name the king associates the remaining hieroglyphs of the cartouche.

The figure with sceptre is the god Amen. On his head he wears a tall hat made up of two long plumes or ostrich feathers. On his chin he wears the long curved beard which indicates his divine nature. A singular custom among the Egyptians was tying a false beard, made of plaited hair, to the end of the chin. It assumed various shapes, to indicate the dignity and position of the wearer. Private individuals wear a small beard about two inches long. That worn by a king was of considerable length, and square at the end; while figures of gods are distinguished by having long beards turned up at the end. The divine beard, the royal beard, and the ordinary beard, are thus easily distinguished.

Amen was the supreme god worshipped at Thebes. He corresponds to Zeus among the Greeks, and Jupiter among the Latins. Rameses associates with his own name that of Amen. The hieroglyphs inside the cartouche are " Ra-mes-es-meri-Amen," which literally translated mean, " Born of Ra, beloved of Amen." The king consequently claims descent from the supreme solar deity of Heliopolis, and the favour of the supreme god of Thebes.

First side.—Left hand.

" Horus, powerful bull, beloved of Ra, lord of Upper and Lower Egypt, lord of festivals, like his father Ptah-Totanen, son of the sun, Rameses-meri-Amen, powerful bull, like the son of Nut ; none can stand before him, lord of the two countries, Ra-user-Ma-sotep-en-Ra, son of the sun, Rameses-meri-Amen."

On the third face, Rameses calls himself the son of Tum, but here he claims Ptah Totanen as his father.

Ptah, also called Ptah Totanen, was the chief god worshipped at Memphis, and is spoken of as the creator of visible things. Tum is also represented as possessing the creative attribute, and it is not improbable that Ptah and Tum sometimes stand for each other. The obelisk stood before the temple of Tum at Heliopolis, and was probably connected with that deity. That Ptah stands for Tum seems to receive confirmation from the fact that after Ptah's name comes the figure of a god used as a determinative. This figure has on its head a solar disk, and therefore appears to be intended for a solar deity.

Nut was a sky-goddess, and represents the blue midday sky. She was said to be the mother of Osiris, who is the friend of mankind, and one of the gods much beloved.

Second side.—Right hand.

" Horus, powerful bull, son of Kheper, king of Upper and Lower Egypt, Ra-user-Ma-sotep-en-Ra, golden hawk, abounding in years, greatly powerful, son of the sun,

Rameses-meri-Amen; the eyes of created beings witness what he has done, nothing has been said against the lord of the two countries, Ra-user-Ma-sotep-en-Ra, son of the sun. Rameses-meri-Amen, the lustre of the son, like the sun."

The *kheper*, or sacred beetle, was sacred to both Ptah and to Tum, and it ought to be observed that Rameses claims each of these gods as his father.

The *hawk* was an emblem of a solar deity, and it was described as golden, in reference to the golden rays of the sun.

The bird at the bottom of this lateral column of hieroglyphs rendered the lustre, is the *bennu*, or sacred bird of Heliopolis, regarded as an incarnation of a solar deity, and therefore the symbol for lustre or splendour. It is often depicted with two long feathers, or one feather, on the back of its head.

Second side.—Left hand.

" Horus, powerful bull, beloved of truth, king of Upper and Lower Egypt, Ra-user-Ma-sotep-en-Ra, born of the gods, holding the country as son of the sun, Rameses-meri-Amen, making his frontiers at the place he wishes— at peace by means of his power, lord of the two countries, Ra-user-Ma-sotep-en-Ra, son of the sun, Rameses-meri-Amen, with splendour like Ra."

In the above *frontier* is represented by a *cross*, to indicate where one country passes into another. The flat land of Egypt is represented by a straight line (*ta*), probably designed to be a layer of earth, while a chip of rock stands for any rocky country, such as Nubia, or for a rocky locality, as Syene, on the frontiers of Nubia, the region of the great granite quarries.   In the column it will be noticed that Rameses vauntingly asserts that his conquests were co-extensive with his desires.

Third side.—Right hand.

"Horus, powerful bull, beloved by Ra, king of Upper and Lower Egypt, Ra–user–Ma–sotep–en–Ra, lord of festivals, like his father Ptah, son of the sun.   Rameses-meri-Amen, son of Tum, out of his loins, loved of him. Hathor, the guide of the two countries, has given birth to him, Ra–user–Ma–sotep–en–Ra, son of the sun, Rameses-meri-Amen, giver of life, like the sun."

In the above, the hieroglyph rendered Hathor is an oblong figure with a small square inscribed in one corner, thus resembling a stamped envelope.   This oblong figure called *ha*, probably represented the ground plan of a temple or house, and is rendered abode, house, temple, or palace, according to the context.   Inside the ground-plan in this case is a figure of a hawk, the emblem of a solar deity.   Here it stands for Horus, and the entire hieroglyph (*ha, hor*) rendered Hathor, means "the abode of Horus."   The "abode of Horus" refers to his mother, a goddess who is therefore named Hathor, or Athor.

The cow is often used as an emblem of this goddess.
Isis also is the reputed mother of Horus, and consequently some think that Hathor and Isis are two
names for one and the same goddess.

Third side.— Left hand.

" Horus, the powerful bull, son of Tum, king of Upper
and Lower Egypt, Ra–user–Ma–sotep–en–Ra, lord of kingly
and queenly royalty, guardian of Egypt, chastiser of
foreign lands, son of the sun. Rameses–meri–Amen,
coming daily into the temple of Tum; he has seen
nothing in the house of his father, lord of the two
countries, Ra-user-Ma-sotep-en-Ra, son of the sun,
Rameses–meri–Amen, like the sun."

In the above the word rendered guardian is *mak*, a
word made up of three phonetic hieroglyphs, namely, a
hole, arm, and semicircle.

Egypt, called *Kham*, that is the black country, is here
represented by a crocodile's tail, since crocodiles were
common in the country, and characteristic of Egypt.

The word rendered chastiser is in the original *auf*, a
name made up of three phonetic hieroglyphs, namely, an
arm, chick, horned snake. The arrangement of these
hieroglyphs with a view to neatness and economising
space displays both taste and ingenuity.

While it is asserted that Rameses went into the
temple of Tum every day, it is also said that he saw
nothing in the temple. This seems like a contradiction;

but, according to classic writers, Rameses II., called by the Greeks Sesostris, became blind in his old age, and the preceding passage may have reference to the monarch's blindness.

Fourth side.—Right hand.

"Horus, powerful bull, beloved of Ra, king of Upper and Lower Egypt, Ra-user-Ma-sotep-en-Ra, the son of Ra, born of the gods, holding his dominions with power, victory, glory ; the bull of princes, king of kings, lord of the two countries, Ra-user-Ma-sotep-en-Ra, son of the sun, Rameses-men-Amen, of Tum, beloved of Heliopolis, giver of life."

In the above, a lion's head, called *peh*, stands for glory, and a crook like that of a shepherd, called *hek*, stands for ruler or prince.

The phrase, "king of kings," occurs in the above, and is the earliest instance of this grand expression—familiar to Christian ears from the fact that in the Bible it is applied to the High and lofty One that inhabiteth eternity. "Alleluia: for the Lord God Omnipotent reigneth .... and on His vesture a name written, KING OF KINGS AND LORD OF LORDS."

Fourth side.—Left hand.

" Horus, powerful bull, son of Truth, king of Upper and Lower Egypt, Ra-user-Ma-sotep-en-Ra, golden hawk,

supplier of years, most powerful son of the sun, Rameses-
meri-Amen, leading captive the Rutennu and Peti out
of their countries to the house of his father; lord of the
two countries, Ra-user-Ma-sotep-en-Ra, son of the sun,
Rameses-meri-Amen, beloved of Shu, great god like the
sun."

The first half of the above is almost identical with the
upper part of the lateral column on the second side
right hand. The *Rutennu* probably mean the Syrians,
and the *Peti* either the Libyans or Nubians.

Shu was a solar deity, the son of Tum.

CHAPTER XIV.

THE RECENT DISCOVERY OF THE MUMMIES OF THOTHMES III. AND RAMESES II. AT DEIR-EL-BAHARI.

IN Cairo, at the Boolak Museum, there is a vast collection of Egyptian antiquities, even more valuable than the collections to be seen at the British Museum, and at the Louvre, Paris. The precious treasures of the Boolak Museum were for the most part collected through the indefatigable labours of the late Mariette Bey. Since his death the charge of the Museum has been entrusted to the two well-known Egyptologists, Professor Maspero and Herr Emil Brugsch.

Professor Maspero lately remarked that for the last ten years he had noticed with considerable astonishment that many valuable Egyptian relics found their way in a mysterious manner to European museums as well as to the private collections of European noblemen. He therefore suspected that the Arabs in the neighbourhood of Thebes, in Upper Egypt, had discovered and were plundering some royal tombs. This suspicion was intensified by the fact that Colin Campbell, on returning to Cairo from a visit to Upper Egypt, showed to the

Professor some pages of a superb royal ritual, purchased from some Arabs at Thebes. M. Maspero accordingly made a journey to Thebes, and on arriving at the place, conferred on the subject with Daoud Pasha, the governor of the district, and offered a handsome reward to any person who would give information of any recently discovered royal tombs.

Behind the ruins of the Ramesseum is a terrace of rock-hewn tombs, occupied by the families of four brothers named Abd-er-Rasoul. The brothers professed to be guides and donkey-masters, but in reality they made their livelihood by tomb-breaking and mummy-snatching. Suspicion at once fell upon them, and a mass of concurrent testimony pointed to the four brothers as the possessors of the secret. With the approval of the district governor, one of the brothers, Ahmed-Abd-er-Rasoul, was arrested and sent to prison at Keneh, the chief town of the district. Here he remained in confinement for two months, and preserved an obstinate silence. At length Mohammed, the eldest brother, fearing that Ahmed's constancy might give way, and fearing lest the family might lose the reward offered by M. Maspero, came to the governor and volunteered to divulge the secret. Having made his depositions, the governor telegraphed to Cairo, whither the Professor had returned. It was felt that no time should be lost. Accordingly M. Maspero empowered Herr Emil Brugsch, keeper of the Boolak Museum, and Ahmed Effendi Kemal, also of the Museum service, to proceed without delay to Upper

Egypt. In a few hours from the arrival of the telegram the Boolak officials were on their way to Thebes. The distance of the journey is about five hundred miles; and as a great part had to be undertaken by the Nile steamer, four days elapsed before they reached their destination, which they did on Wednesday, 6th July, 1881.

On the western side of the Theban plain rises a high mass of limestone rock, enclosing two desolate valleys. One runs up behind the ridge into the very heart of the hills, and being entirely shut in by the limestone cliffs, is a picture of wild desolation. The other valley runs up from the plain, and its mouth opens out towards the city of Thebes. "The former is the Valley of the Tombs of the Kings—the Westminster Abbey of Thebes; the latter, of the Tombs of the Priests and Princes—its Canterbury Cathedral." High up among the limestone cliffs, and near the plateau overlooking the plain of Thebes, is the site of an old temple, known as "Deir-el-Bahari."

At this last-named place, according to agreement, the Boolak officials met Mohammed Abd-er-Rasoul, a spare, sullen fellow, who simply from love of gold had agreed to divulge the grand secret. Pursuing his way among desecrated tombs, and under the shadow of precipitous cliffs, he led his anxious followers to a spot described as ' unparalleled, even in the desert, for its gaunt solemnity." Here, behind a huge fragment of fallen rock, perhaps dislodged for that purpose from the cliffs overhead, they

H

were shown the entrance to a pit so ingeniously hidden that, to use their own words, "one might have passed it twenty times without observing it." The shaft of the pit proved to be six and a-half feet square; and on being lowered by means of a rope, they touched the ground at a depth of about forty feet.

Truth is sometimes stranger than fiction, and certainly nothing in romantic literature can surpass in dramatic interest the revelation which awaited the Boolak officials in the subterranean sepulchral chambers of Deir-el-Bahari. At the bottom of the shaft the explorers noticed a dark passage running westward; so, having lit their candles, they groped their way slowly along the passage, which ran in a straight line for twenty-three feet, and then turned abruptly to the right, stretching away northward into total darkness. At the corner where the passage turned northward, they found a royal funeral canopy, flung carelessly down in a tumbled heap. As they proceeded, they found the roof so low in some places that they were obliged to stoop, and in other parts the rocky floor was very uneven. At a distance of sixty feet from the corner, the explorers found themselves at the top of a flight of stairs, roughly hewn out of the rock. Having descended the steps, each with his flickering candle in hand, they pursued their way along a passage slightly descending, and penetrating deeper and further into the heart of the mountain. As they proceeded, the floor became more and more strewn with fragments of mummy cases and tattered pieces of mummy bandages.

Presently they noticed boxes piled on the top of each other against the wall, and these boxes proved to be filled with porcelain statuettes, libation jars, and canopic vases of precious alabaster. Then appeared several huge coffins of painted wood; and great was their joy when they gazed upon a crowd of mummy cases, some standing, some laid upon the ground, each fashioned in human form, with folded hands and solemn faces. On the breast of each was emblazoned the name and titles of the occupant. Words fail to describe the joyous excitement of the scholarly explorers, when among the group they read the names of Seti I., Thothmes II., Thothmes III., and Rameses II., surnamed the Great.

The Boolak officials had journeyed to Thebes, expecting at most to find a few mummies of petty princes; but on a sudden they were brought, as it were, face to face with the mightiest kings of ancient Egypt, and confronted the remains of heroes whose exploits and fame filled the ancient world with awe more than three thousand years ago.

The explorers stood bewildered, and could scarcely believe the testimony of their own eyes, and actually inquired of each other if they were not in a dream. At the end of a passage, one hundred and thirty feet from the bottom of the rock-cut passage, they stood at the entrance of a sepulchral chamber, twenty-three feet long, and thirteen feet wide, literally piled to the roof with mummy cases of enormous size. The coffins were brilliant with colour-gilding and varnish, and looked as fresh as if they had recently come out of the workshops of the Memnonium.

Among the mummies of this mortuary chapel were found two kings, four queens, a prince and a princess, besides royal and priestly personages of both sexes, all descendants of Her-Hor, the founder of the line of priest-kings known as the XXIst dynasty. The chamber was manifestly the family vault of the Her-Hor family; while the mummies of their more illustrious predecessors of the XVIIIth and XIXth dynasties, found in the approaches to the chamber, had evidently been brought there for the sake of safety. Each member of the family was buried with the usual mortuary outfit. One queen, named Isi-em-Kheb (Isis of Lower Egypt), was also provided with a sumptuous funereal repast, as well as a rich sepulchral toilet, consisting of ointment bottles, alabaster cups, goblets of exquisite variegated glass, and a large assortment of full dress wigs, curled and frizzed. As the funereal repast was designed for refreshment, so the sepulchral toilet was designed for the queen's use and adornment on the Resurrection morn, when the vivified dead, clothed, fed, anointed and perfumed, should leave the dark sepulchral chamber and go forth to the mansions of everlasting day.

When the temporary excitement of the explorers had somewhat abated, they felt that no time was to be lost in securing their newly discovered treasures. Accordingly, three hundred Arabs were engaged from the neighbouring villages; and working as they did with unabated

vigour, without sleep and without rest, they succeeded
in clearing out the sepulchral chamber and the long
passages of their valuable contents in the short space of
forty-eight hours.   All the mummies were then carefully
packed in sail-cloth and matting, and carried across the
plain of Thebes to the edge of the river.   Thence they
were rowed across the Nile to Luxor, there to lie in
readiness for embarkation on the approach of the Nile
steamers.

Some of the sarcophagi are of huge dimensions, the
largest being that of Nofretari, a queen of the XVIIIth
dynasty.   The coffin is ten feet long, made of cartonnage,
and in style resembles one of the Osiride pillars of the
Temple of Medinat Aboo.   Its weight and size are so
enormous that sixteen men were required to remove it.
In spite of all difficulties, however, only five days elapsed
from the time the Boolak officials were lowered down
the shaft until the precious relics lay ready for embarkation at Luxor.

The Nile steamers did not arrive for three days, and
during that time Messrs. Brugsch and Kemal, and a
few trustworthy Arabs, kept constant guard over their
treasure amid a hostile fanatical people who regarded
tomb-breaking as the legitimate trade of the neighbourhood.   On the fourth morning the steamers arrived, and
having received on board the royal mummies, steamed
down the stream *en route* for the Boolak Muscum.
Meanwhile the news of the discovery had spread far
and wide, and for fifty miles below Luxor, the villagers

lined the river banks, not merely to catch a glimpse of the mummies on deck as the steamers passed by, but also to show respect for the mighty dead. Women with dishevelled hair ran along the banks shrieking the death-wail; while men stood in solemn silence, and fired guns into the air to greet the mighty Pharaohs as they passed. Thus, to the mummified bodies of Thothmes the Great, and Rameses the Great, and their illustrious compeers, the funeral honours paid to them three thousand years ago were, in a measure, repeated as the mortal remains of these ancient heroes sailed down the Nile on their way to Boolak.

The principal personages found either as mummies, or represented by their mummy cases, include a king and queen of the XVIIth dynasty, five kings and four queens of the XVIIIth dynasty, and three successive kings of the XIXth dynasty, namely, Rameses the Great, his father, and his grandfather. The XXth dynasty, strange to say, is not represented; but belonging to the XXIst dynasty of royal priests are four queens, two kings, a prince, and a princess.

These royal mummies belong to four dynasties, and between the earliest and the latest there intervenes a period of above seven centuries,—a space of time as long as that which divides the Norman Conquest from the accession of George III. Under the dynasties above mentioned ancient Egypt reached the summit of her fame, through the expulsion of the Hykshos invaders, and the extensive conquests of Thothmes III.

and Rameses the Great. The oppression of Israel in Egypt and the Exodus of the Hebrews, the colossal temples of Thebes, the royal sepulchres of the Valley of the Tombs of the Kings, the greater part of the Pharaonic obelisks, and the rock-cut temples of the Nile Valley, belong to the same period.

It would be beyond the scope of this brief account to describe each royal personage, and therefore there can only be given a short description of the two kings connected with the London Obelisk, namely, Thothmes III. and Rameses the Great, the mightiest of the Pharaohs.

Standing near the end of the long dark passage running northward, and not far from the threshold of the family vault of the priest-kings, lay the sarcophagus of Thothmes III., close to that of his brother Thothmes II. The mummy case was in a lamentable condition, and had evidently been broken into and subjected to rough usage. On the lid, however, were recognized the well-known cartouches of this illustrious monarch. On opening the coffin, the mummy itself was exposed to view, completely enshrouded with bandages; but a rent near the left breast showed that it had been exposed to the violence of tomb-breakers. Placed inside the coffin and surrounding the body were found wreaths of flowers: larkspurs, acacias and lotuses. They looked as if but recently dried, and even their colours could be discerned.

Long hieroglyphic texts found written on the bandages contained the seventeenth chapter of the " Ritual of the Dead," and the " Litanies of the Sun."

The body measured only five feet two inches; so that, making due allowance for shrinking and compression in the process of embalming, still it is manifest that Thothmes III. was not a man of commanding stature; but in shortness of stature as in brilliancy of conquests, finds his counterpart in the person of Napoleon the Great.

It was desirable in the interests of science to ascertain whether the mummy bearing the monogram of Thothmes III. was really the remains of that monarch. It was therefore unrolled. The inscriptions cn the bandages established beyond all doubt the fact that it was indeed the most distinguished of the kings of the brilliant XVIIIth dynasty; and once more, after an interval of thirty-six centuries, human eyes gazed on the features of the man who had conquered Syria, and Cyprus, and Ethiopia, and had raised Egypt to the highest pinnacle of her power; so that it was said that in his reign she placed her frontiers where she pleased. The spectacle was of brief duration; the remains proved to be in so fragile a state that there was only time to take a hasty photograph, and then the features crumbled to pieces and vanished like an apparition, and so passed away from human view for ever. The director felt such remorse at the result that he refused to allow the unrolling of Rameses the Great, for fear of a similar catastrophe.

Thothmes III. was the man who overran Palestine with his armies two hundred years before the birth of Moses, and has left us a diary of his adventures; for, like Cæsar, he was author as well as soldier. It seems strange that though the body mouldered to dust, the flowers with which it had been wreathed were so wonderfully preserved, that even their colour could be distinguished; yet a flower is the very type of ephemeral beauty, that passeth away and is gone almost as soon as born. A wasp which had been attracted by the floral treasures, and had entered the coffin at the moment of closing, was found dried up, but still perfect, having lasted better than the king whose emblem of sovereignty it had once been; now it was there to mock the embalmer's skill, and to add point to the sermon on the vanity of human pride and power preached to us by the contents of that coffin. Inexorable is the decree, "Unto dust thou shalt return."

Following the same line of meditation, it is difficult to avoid a thought of the futility of human devices to achieve immortality. These Egyptian monarchs, the veriest type of earthly grandeur and pride, whose rule was almost limitless, whose magnificent tombs seem built to outlast the hills, could find no better method of ensuring that their names should be had in remembrance than the embalmment of their frail bodies. These remain, but in what a condition, and how degraded are the uses to which they are put. The spoil of an ignorant and thieving population, the pet curiosity of some wealthy tourist, who buys a royal mummy as he would buy the Sphinx, if it were moveable; "to what base uses art thou come," O body, so tenderly nurtured, so carefully preserved!

Rameses II. died about thirteen centuries before the Christian era. It is certain that this illustrious monarch was originally buried in the stately tomb of the magnificent subterranean sepulchre by royal order hewn out of the limestone cliffs in the Valley of the Tombs of the Kings. In the same valley his grandfather and father were laid to rest ; so that these three mighty kings " all lay in glory, each in his own house." This burial-place of the Pharaohs of the XVIIIth and XIXth dynasties is in a deep gorge behind the western hills of the Theban plain. " The valley is the very ideal of desolation. Bare rocks, without a particle of vegetation, overhanging and enclosing in a still narrower and narrower embrace a valley as rocky and bare as themselves—no human habitation visible—the stir of the city wholly excluded. Such is, such always must have been, the awful aspect of the resting-place of the Theban kings. The sepulchres of this valley are of extraordinary grandeur. You enter a sculptured portal in the face of these wild cliffs, and find yourself in a long and lofty gallery, opening or narrowing, as the case may be, into successive halls and chambers, all of which are covered with white stucco, and this white stucco, brilliant with colours, fresh as they were thousands of years ago. The sepulchres are in fact gorgeous palaces, hewn out of the rock, and painted with all the decorations that could have been seen in palaces."

One of the most gorgeous of these sepulchral palaces was that prepared in this valley by Rameses II., and after the burial of the king the portals were walled up, and the mummified body laid to rest in the vaulted hall till the morn of the Resurrection. From a hieratic inscription found on the mummy-case of Rameses, it appears that official Inspectors of Tombs visited this royal tomb in the sixth year of Her-Hor, the founder of the priestly line of kings; so that for at least two centuries the mummy of Rameses the Great lay undisturbed in the original tomb prepared for its reception. From several papyri still extant, it appears that the neighbourhood of Thebes at this period, and for many years previously, was in a state of social insecurity. Lawlessness, rapine and tomb-breaking, filled the whole district with alarm. The "Abbott Papyrus" states that royal sepulchres were broken open, cleared of mummies, jewels, and all their contents. In the "Amherst Papyrus," a lawless tomb-breaker, in relating how he broke into a royal sepulchre, makes the following confession :—"The tomb was surrounded by masonry, and covered in by roofing-stones. We demolished it, and found the king and queen reposing therein. We found the august king with his divine axe beside him, and his amulets and ornaments of gold about his neck. His head was covered with gold, and his august person was entirely covered with gold. His coffins were overlaid with gold and silver, within and without, and incrusted with all kinds of precious stones. We took the gold which we found upon the sacred person of this god, as also his amulets, and the ornaments which were about his neck and the coffins in which he reposed. And having likewise found his royal wife, we took all that we found upon her in the same manner; and we set fire to their mummy cases, and we seized upon their furniture, their vases of gold, silver, and bronze, and we divided them amongst ourselves."

Such being the dreadful state of insecurity during the latter period of the XXth dynasty, and throughout the whole of the Her-Hor dynasty, we are not surprised to find that the mummy of Rameses II., and that of his grandfather, Rameses I., were removed for the sake of greater security from their own separate catacombs into the tomb of his father Seti I. In the sixteenth year of Her-Hor, that is, ten years after the official inspection mentioned above, a commission of priests visited the three royal mummies in the tomb of Seti. On an entry found on the mummy case of Seti and Rameses II., the priests certify that the bodies are in an uninjured condition; but they deemed it expedient, on grounds of safety, to transfer the three mummies to the tomb of Ansera, a queen of the XVIIth dynasty. For ten years at least Rameses' body reposed in this abode; but in the tenth year of Pinotem was removed into "the eternal house of Amen-hotep." A fourth inscription on the breast bandages of Rameses relates how that after resting for six years the body was again carried back to the tomb of his father in "the Valley of the Tombs of the Kings," a valley now called "Bab-el-Molook."

How long the body remained in this resting-place, and how many transfers it was subsequently subjected to, there exists no evidence to show ; but after being exposed to many vicissitudes, the mummy of Rameses, together with those of his royal relatives, and many of his illustrious predecessors, was brought in as a refugee into the family vault of the Her-Hor dynasty. In this subterranean hiding-place, buried deep in the heart of the Theban Hills, Rameses the Great, surrounded by a goodly company of thirty royal mummies, lay undisturbed and unseen by mortal eye for three thousand years, until, a few years ago, the lawless tomb-breakers of Thebes burrowed into this sepulchral chamber.

The mummy-case containing Rameses' mummy is not the original one, for it belongs to the style of the XXIst dynasty, and was probably made at the time of the official inspection of his tomb in the sixth year of Her-Hor's reign. It is made of unpainted sycamore wood, and the lid is of the shape known as Osirian, that is, the deceased is represented in the well-known attitude of Osiris, with arms crossed, and hands grasping a crook and flail. The eyes are inserted in enamel, while the eyebrows, eyelashes, and beard are painted black. Upon the breast are the familiar cartouches of Rameses II., namely, *Ra-user-Ma-sotep-en-Ra*, his prenomen ; and *Ra-me-su-Meri-amen*, his nomen.

The mummy itself is in good condition, and measures six feet ; but as in the process of mummification the larger bones were probaby drawn closer together in their sockets, its seems self-evident that Rameses was a man of commanding appearance. It is thus satisfactory to learn that the mighty Sesostris was a hero of great physical stature, that this conqueror of Palestine was in height equal to a grenadier.

The outer shrouds of the body are made of rose-coloured linen, and bound together by very strong bands. Within the outer shrouds, the mummy is swathed in its original bandages ; and Professor Maspero has expressed his intention of removing these inner bandages on some convenient opportunity, in the presence of scholars and medical witnesses.

It has been urged that since Rameses XII., of the XXth dynasty, had a prenomen similar though not identical with the divine cartouche of Rameses II., the mummy in question may be that of Rameses XII. We have, however, shown that the mummies of Rameses I., Seti I., and Rameses II., were exposed to the same vicissitudes, buried, transferred, and reburied again and again in the same vaults. When, therefore, we find in the sepulchre at Deir-el-Bahari, in juxta-position, the mummy-case of Rameses I., the mummy-case and acknowledged mummy of Seti I., and on the mummy-case and shroud the well-known cartouches of Rameses II., the three standing in the relation of grand-father, father, and son, it seems that the evidence is overwhelming in favour of the mummy in question being that of Rameses the Great.

All the royal mummies, twenty-nine in number, are now lying in state in the Boolak Museum. Arranged together side by side and shoulder to shoulder, they form a solemn assembly of kings, queens, royal priests, princes, princesses, and nobles of the people.   Among the group are the mummied remains of the greatest royal builders, the most renowned warriors, and mightiest monarchs of ancient Egypt.   They speak to us of the military glory and architectural splendour of that marvellous country thirty-five centuries ago ; they illustrate the truth of the words of the Christian Apostle : " All flesh is as grass, and all the glory of man as the flower of grass.   The grass withereth, and the flower thereof falleth away : but the word of the Lord endureth for ever.   And this is the word which by the Gospel is preached unto you."*

These great Egyptian rulers, in all their magnificence and power, had no Gospel in their day, and can preach no Gospel to those who gaze wonderingly upon their remains, so strangely brought to light.   Much as we should like to hear the tale they could unfold of a civilization of which we seem to know so much, and yet in reality know so little, on all these questions they are for ever silent.   But they utter a weighty message to all whose temptation now is to lose sight of the future in the present, of the eternal by reason of the temporal.   They show how fleeting and unsubstantial are even the highest earthly rank and wealth and in- fluence ; and how true is the lesson taught by him who knew all that Egypt could teach, and much that God could reveal, and whose life is interpreted for us by the writer of the Epistle to the Hebrews : " By faith Moses,

* 1 Peter i. 24, 25.

when he was come to years, refused to be called the son of Pharaoh's daughter; choosing rather to suffer affliction with the people of God, than to enjoy the pleasures of sin for a season; esteeming the reproach of Christ greater riches than the treasures in Egypt: for he had respect unto the recompence of the reward." *

* Heb. xi. 24-26.

Harrison and Sons, Printers in Ordinary to Her Majesty, St. Martin's Lane, London

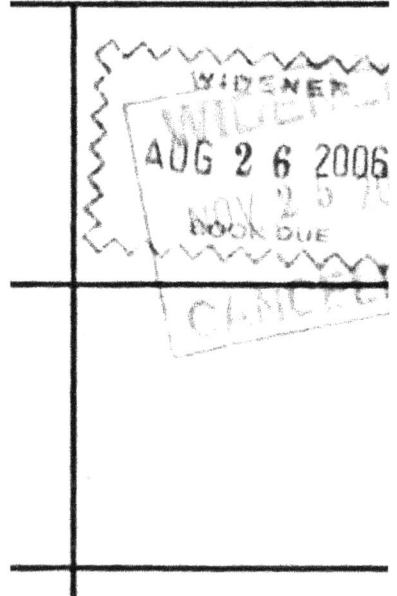

Printed in Dunstable, United Kingdom